CYLINDRICAL STEMS

SEGMENTED STEMS

STICK-LIKE STEMS

COLUMNAR STEMS

Cacti *of* Arizona

Field Guide

Nora and Rick Bowers
Stan Tekiela

Adventure PUBLICATIONS
an imprint of AdventureKEEN

Our enduring gratitude to Matt Johnson, our good friend and cactus guru, for his patient tutoring over the years. Maybe one day it will stick. — Nora and Rick

ACKNOWLEDGMENTS

We thank Kerry and Kim Bergman for their generosity and support, without which this book would not have been possible. Thanks to Cathryn Hoyt and Marc Goff at the Chihuahuan Desert Nature Center, Fort Davis, Texas, for their help and allowing photography of their cacti. We are also grateful to those people and institutions responsible for the Flora of North America and SEI Net web sites, for making scientific information accessible to all. Special thanks to Matt Johnson for reviewing the range maps, suggesting locations for photography and answering taxonomic questions based on his extensive knowledge of Arizona's cacti.

Edited by Sandy Livoti

Contributing Editors: Brett Ortler and Deborah Walsh

Cover and book design by Jonathan Norberg

Cactus illustrations by Julie Martinez

Range maps produced by Anthony Hertzel

Photo credits: Cover photo by LHBLLC/Shutterstock. See pages 232–233 for photo credits by photographer and page number.

10 9 8 7 6 5 4 3 2 1

Cacti of Arizona Field Guide
First Edition 2008
Second Edition 2023
Copyright © 2008 and 2023 by Nora and Rick Bowers and Stan Tekiela
Published by Adventure Publications
An imprint of AdventureKEEN
310 Garfield Street South
Cambridge, Minnesota 55008
(800) 678-7006
www.adventurepublications.net
All rights reserved
Printed in China
Cataloging-in-Publication data is available from the Library of Congress
ISBN 978-1-64755-397-5 (pbk.); ISBN 978-1-64755-398-2 (ebook)

TABLE OF CONTENTS

ARIZONA AND CACTI

Arizona is a great place for anyone who loves plants—especially those interested in cacti! From the hot arid deserts of the south to the colder desert habitats and grasslands of the north, Arizona is fortunate to have extremely diverse, often unique, and beautiful cacti.

Cacti of Arizona Field Guide is designed to help the curious nature seeker easily identify 50 of the most common and widespread cactus species in Arizona. It is a photo-driven guide just for Arizona, featuring full-color images of entire cacti, close-ups of cactus spines, vivid flowers, fruit, and more. It is one in a series of unique field guides for Arizona, including those for birds, mammals, trees, and wildflowers.

WHAT IS A CACTUS?

Cacti are succulents—drought-tolerant plants that store large quantities of water in their fleshy (succulent) leaves, stems or roots. There are many families of succulent plants, differing mainly in the structure of their flowers. Cacti are members of one succulent family, the *Cactaceae*. So, although all cacti are succulents, not all succulents are cacti.

For the purposes of this book, a cactus is defined as having fleshy, leafless stems with waxy, water-retaining skin, and prickly spines emerging in clusters from specialized areas in the skin called areoles. Food production (photosynthesis) in cacti is mainly accomplished in the stems by enlarged green cells that also retain water. Spines provide shade for the stems, reducing water evaporation, and form a barrier that defends the plant from being eaten by animals. Cactus flowers are usually handsome, with many similar-looking petals and petal-like sepals, hundreds of pollen-bearing male flower parts (stamens), and several sticky female flower parts (stigmas). *Cacti of Arizona Field Guide* will help you observe stems, spines, flowers, and other basic characteristics so you can confidently identify different species.

IDENTIFICATION STEP-BY-STEP

In this field guide, cacti are organized by overall plant or stem shape. To aid identification, we've divided the cacti into four general shape categories, and each shape has a color-coded thumb tab in the upper right hand corner of the first description pages. We've included four different categories: short cacti with cylindrical stems (maroon tab), cacti with segmented stems (green tab), cacti with very thin, stick-like stems (gold tab), and tall cacti with columnar stems (blue tab).

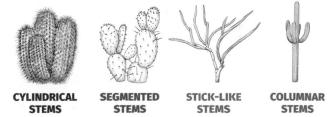

| CYLINDRICAL STEMS | SEGMENTED STEMS | STICK-LIKE STEMS | COLUMNAR STEMS |

SUBCATEGORIES

Each stem shape is broken down into additional subcategories, and each subcategory has a corresponding icon that is immediately below the color-coded shape icon. Cacti with similar subcategories are grouped together, and each section is loosely organized by stem size from small to large. This can be helpful when the plant you are trying to identify is at its mature height. The measurement given for each species is the typical height of the cactus as it is most

commonly seen, with a few exceptions. Cacti vary throughout the year, shrinking during drought and cold, and gaining
height and girth during the rainy season.

The Cylindrical Stem Group

If a mature cactus is under 5 feet (1.5 m) tall and has cylindrical stems, it belongs in this short cacti group. The next
step is to identify whether it is a pincushion, pineapple-
beehive, hedgehog, or barrel cactus. Each of these four types
of cacti is represented by a unique icon in the thumb tabs.

 Pincushion cacti are the shortest, roundest cacti,
and the stems usually grow in clusters. Firm
conical knobs, called tubercles, spiral around the
stems. Tubercles are topped with a spine cluster
of fine spines, sometimes shaped like fishhooks. Flowers
appear in a ring at the top of the stems. Pincushion fruit
lacks hair, scales, or spines.

 Pineapple and beehive cacti appear so similar
that they are combined into one section with one
thumb tab icon. Pineapple cacti are pineapple-
shaped short plants, but vary in shape from
somewhat globe-shaped to cylindrical. They usually have
a single stem (sometimes small clusters) with tubercles
arranged on vertical ribs rather than in spirals. Blossoms
are short, stiff, funnel-shaped, and appear in dense tufts at
the tip of stems. Fruit is fleshy and scaly, drying when ripe in
most species. Beehive cacti have globe-shaped stems with a
flat top, much like a honeybee hive. Cone-shaped tubercles
on the skin appear in spirals. Each tubercle has a groove on
the upper side and a cluster of spines growing from the tip.
Beehive cacti often grow as one stem, but some species
appear in large clusters. While similar to pincushion cacti,
beehives differ because of the tubercle grooves, stouter

spines, longer taproots, and flowers that are densely clustered on top of the stems.

 Hedgehog cacti are taller and therefore appear slimmer than pincushions. Stems have vertical folds of ridges and grooves (called ribs) and often grow in clusters. Large flowers bloom just below the tip of stems, emerging through the skin above a mature spine cluster. The fruit of hedgehog cacti is spiny.

 Barrel cacti are the largest of the cylindrical cacti, with thick, barrel-shaped stems under 5 feet (1.5 m). Stem surfaces are ribbed and lined with spine clusters. Most barrel cacti grow as single-stemmed plants; however, the Many-headed Barrel cactus branches into clusters of stems.

The Segmented Stem Group

Segmented cacti are shrubby or tree-like. In this type of cactus, new stem segments, or joints, branch from the previous year's segments. Beginning as buds with tiny leaves, these grow and divide during the rainy season before growing spines. In addition to the usual spines, spine clusters have many tiny barbed bristles known as glochids. Prickly glochids are more easily felt than seen and present only in prickly pear and cholla cacti. There are two main types of cacti with segmented stems and each group is represented by its own thumb tab icon.

 Prickly pears have flat, paddle-shaped stems.

 Chollas, on the other hand, are cacti with slender cylindrical stems.

The Stick-like Stem Group

 Only cacti in the *Peniocereus* genus have thin stick-like stems, which are either squared or rounded. Desert Night-blooming Cereus, the most common stick-like cactus in Arizona, is represented by its own thumb tab icon. This species has large white flowers that bloom during a single night.

The Columnar Stem Group

Cacti with stems shaped like columns can be as large as some trees at maturity. Stem surfaces have ribbed ridges and grooves. Large white or pink-tinged blossoms emerge from spine clusters or below the tip of stems and open at night. Their fruit is large, oblong, and mostly smooth. The three columnar cacti in this book are distinguished from each other by their spines and flowers. Each species is represented by individual thumb tab icons and each icon is shown below.

 Organ Pipe Cactus has many slim round columns of vertically ribbed stems branching from the base.

Senita Cactus has many 6–sided columns branching from the base with beard-like gray spines topping the older stems.

Saguaro Cactus has a large, telephone pole-like stem (trunk) with gracefully curving arms branching from the upper trunk.

USING PHOTOS TO CONFIRM THE IDENTITY

After using the thumb tabs to narrow your choices, the last step is to confirm the identity of the cactus. First, compare it with the photos of entire plants and consider the information given about habitat and consult the range maps. Next, examine the spines and compare them with the inset photos. Since flowers or fruit can be a better indicator of a species, compare those photos as well. Use the rulers on page 236 to help estimate spine, flower and fruit sizes. Finally, look at the three photos above the Compare section to verify the identity of your cactus. These photos illustrate characteristics that differ among similar species.

Or, if you think you know which cactus you're looking for, use the index. In addition, a special cactus-like species section on pages 222–225 includes photos and general information for four common succulent species that can be mistakenly identified as a cactus.

SEASON OF BLOOM

Many cacti have a specific season of blooming. For example, you probably won't see the spring-blooming Beavertail Prickly Pear flowering during summer or autumn. Knowing the season of bloom can help you narrow your selection as you try to identify a cactus. Since seasons in Arizona change at different times at various elevations, we have identified the months in which a cactus normally blooms. Spring usually occurs from the second half of March through May, although some species, such as Woven-spine Pineapple Cactus, bloom as early as February. Summer refers to June, July, and August. Fall usually means September, October, and November.

Some cacti do not bloom during a certain season, but flower anytime it rains in the warmer months. Interestingly, you must look for some cactus flowers at certain times of the day or night. For instance, Desert Christmas Cholla blooms only from four o'clock in the afternoon until after dark. Other cacti, such as Robust-spine Beehive Cactus, bloom for just one day a year, not all individuals on the same day of course.

LIFE ZONES/HABITATS

Sometimes noting the life zone or habitat of a cactus in question can help determine its identity. Ecologists define nine distinct life zones in Arizona. One is subalpine—where no cacti grow. Another, riparian deciduous, occurs within all other zones, but only near streams and intermittently running washes. In this book, for simplicity, five zones are referenced. Elevation, temperature, and annual rainfall distinguish each zone, with shared elevations sometimes resulting in zone overlap. While some cacti are found only in one life zone, others can be seen in several zones or even in all five.

The **desert scrub** life zone is found between 500–6,500 feet (150–1,980 m), but this habitat is defined more by its meager annual rainfall of less than 12 inches (30 cm). It is a unique zone that supports a wide variety of cacti, from the tiny Arizona Fishhook Pincushion to the giant Saguaro, which can grow as tall as a telephone pole. The dominant species of cacti in desert scrub changes with the type of desert and its location in Arizona. Most cactus species in the state grow in desert scrub and grasslands life zones, described next. Others, such as Compass Barrel and Jumping Cholla, are found only in desert scrub.

At some elevations, the **grasslands** life zone mixes with desert scrub habitat or replaces it. Grasslands range between 3,000–7,000 feet (915–2,135 m) and rainfall averages 17 inches

(43 cm) or less per year. Pure grasslands have mostly shrubless stands of grasses with scattered evergreen oak and mesquite trees. This zone suffers from introduced exotic grasses and overgrazing by cattle. While most Arizona cacti are found in this zone as well as in desert scrub, only Wovenspine Pineapple Cactus grows mainly in grasslands.

The **oak/pinyon pine/juniper woodlands** life zone occurs at elevations between 4,000–7,000 feet (1,220–2,135 m), with yearly rainfall averaging 12–24 inches (30–61 cm). Sometimes this habitat overlaps with the grasslands, where trees are widely spaced. Several pinyon pine and evergreen juniper tree species grow in northern Arizona in this zone. In southern Arizona, a mix of evergreen oaks and pinyon pines is predominant, with Spineless Prickly Pear growing among the oaks.

Running roughly east to west in a broken band just south of the Grand Canyon's South Rim lies the **interior chaparral** life zone. Its elevation ranges from 3,000–8,000 feet (915–2,440 m) and annual rainfall averages 15–25 inches (38–64 cm). Interior chaparral is a unique, dense community of deeply rooted evergreen shrubs and trees that regrow easily in a habitat defined by frequent fires. Bonker Hedgehog is common in this life zone.

Elevations are higher in the **montane** life zone, between 6,000–9,000 feet (1,830–2,745 m), and annual rainfall is also increased, averaging between 20–30 inches (50–76 cm). Ponderosa Pine trees dominate the open, park-like forests in this zone and sometimes mix with fir trees on the cooler, moister, north-facing slopes. Meadows near forests with conifers, oaks, maples, and aspens provide a rich environment for a few cold-tolerant cacti such as Kingcup Hedgehog and Spinystar.

Range

The wide variety of life zones in Arizona naturally restricts the range of certain cacti that have specific requirements. Sometimes this section can help you eliminate a cactus from consideration based solely on its range. However, please keep in mind that the ranges indicate where the cactus is most commonly found. They are general guidelines only and there will certainly be exceptions to these ranges.

Compare

Look-alike cacti can be difficult to tell apart. Three comparison photos at the top of description pages draw your attention to differing details of similar-looking species. To help you identify your cactus, the accompanying text contrasts these features and other attributes. Much of the detailed information in this section is unique and not illustrated in other cactus field guides.

Notes

The Notes are fun and fact-filled with many gee-whiz tidbits of interesting information such as historical uses, other common names, relationship of the species with insects, color variations, and much more.

CAUTION

In the Notes, it is occasionally mentioned that parts of some cacti were used for medicine or food. While some find this interesting, DO NOT use this field guide to identify edible or medicinal plants. Please enjoy the cacti of Arizona with your eyes or with your camera. In addition, please don't pick cactus flowers or fruit, cut stems, or attempt to transplant any cacti. The flower of a plant is its reproductive structure, and if you pick a cactus flower you have limited its ability to reproduce. Transplanting cacti is another destructive occurrence. Most cacti need specific soil types, pH and moisture levels, or temperatures to grow properly. If you attempt to transplant a cactus to a habitat that is not suitable for its particular needs, the plant most likely will die.

All cacti in Arizona are protected and can be salvaged or transplanted only by permit, even on private land. Some rare species, due to their dwindling populations, are protected by laws that forbid you to disturb the plants in any way. The good news is many of our cacti in Arizona are now available at local garden centers. These plants have been cultivated and have not been taken from the wild except by permit. Cacti are an important part of our natural environment, and leaving them healthy and unharmed will do a great deal to help keep the Grand Canyon State the exceptional place it is.

Enjoy the Wild Cacti!

Nora, Rick, and Stan

CACTUS BASICS

It's easier to identify cacti and discuss them when you know the names of their different parts. For instance, it is more effective to use the word "glochids" to indicate hair-like spines than to try to describe them. The following illustrations point out the basic parts of various cacti. These are for informational purposes only and should not be confused with any specific cactus species.

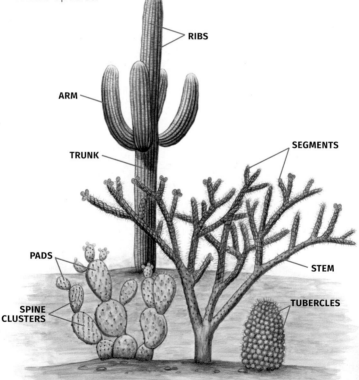

RIBS

ARM

SEGMENTS

TRUNK

PADS

STEM

SPINE CLUSTERS

TUBERCLES

Spine Cluster

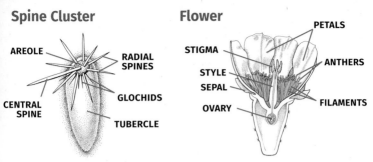

AREOLE

RADIAL SPINES

CENTRAL SPINE

GLOCHIDS

TUBERCLE

Flower

PETALS

STIGMA

ANTHERS

STYLE

SEPAL

OVARY

FILAMENTS

STIGMA + STYLE = **PISTIL**
ANTHERS + FILAMENTS = **STAMENS**

Stems

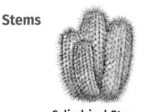

Cylindrical Stems
pincushion, pineapple-beehive, hedgehog, and barrel

Segmented Stems
prickly pear and cholla

Stick-like Stems
Desert Night-blooming Cereus

Columnar Stems
Organ Pipe, Senita, and Saguaro

spines

flower

fruit

Group Color Tab

GROUP

Common Name

Range Map *Scientific Name* Shape

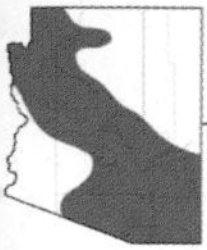

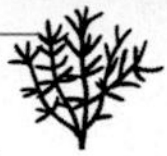

Size: (H) average height of the mature cactus from ground to top; (W) average width of the mature cactus, for those occurring as a single stem

Shape: growth form and overall appearance, may include average width of a cluster of stems

Stem: number of stems and features such as color, stem segment size, or protuberances (tubercles); may include other pertinent details

Spines: color and length

Spine Clusters: number of spines per cluster; brief description of central spines, radial spines, and glochids

Flower: shape, color, position, and size of flower or flower cluster

Blooming: months when the flower blooms; may include related information

Fruit: overall description of pod such as shape, color, size, spines, protuberances (tubercles), edibility, seeds, or attachment

Sample page

Description pages have one of the below designations to indicate the stem shape. See pages 7–10 for more information about stems.

skeleton

Zone/Habitat: desert scrub, grasslands, oak/pinyon pine/juniper woodlands, interior chaparral, and/or montane life zones along with elevation ranges; places where the cactus grows such as desert flats, canyons, valleys, clearings, plateaus, ridges, slopes, hilltops, outcrops, along washes, soil types

Range: parts of Arizona where the cactus is found

 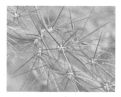 

Main species
description of features
shown in the image

Compare species *(page)*
contrasting description
of features

Compare species *(page)*
contrasting description
of other features

Compare: Notes about other species that look similar and the pages on which they can be found. Up-close color photos show differences among stems, spines, tubercles, flowers, fruit, or other key plant characteristics.

Notes: Helpful identification information such as remarkable features, history, ethnobotanical information, name origins, and other interesting gee-whiz nature facts.

spines

flower

fruit

Heyder Pincushion
Mammillaria heyderi

Size: H ¼–1" (.6–2.5 cm); W 3–6" (7.5–15 cm)

Shape: low-growing, disk-shaped cactus with a flat top

Stem: single stem covered with conical green bumps (tubercles), each topped with a cluster of spines; stem has a milky white sap

Spines: grayish white or pinkish brown with dark tips, ⅕–⁷⁄₁₀" (.5–1.8 cm) long

Spine Clusters: 10–22 spines per cluster; each cluster has 1 short rigid outward-pointing central spine within a semicircle of needle-like radial spines hugging the stem; lowest radials are longest

Flower: small cream or pinkish blossoms in a ring at the top of stem; each flower, 1–1½" (2.5–4 cm) wide, has a wide brownish green or pink stripe on the petals, and a pink and green center

Blooming: March–April

Fruit: conical green pod, ½–1⅜" (1–3.5 cm) long, with fleshy walls and tiny reddish brown seeds, ripens 6 months to a year after blooming, elongating into a cylindrical red pod

Zone/Habitat: higher desert scrub and grasslands from 3,500–6,000' (1,065–1,830 m); rocky limestone hills, washes, among grasses, or under shrubs

Range: southeastern corner of Arizona, from the junction of Highway 83 and Interstate 10 (east of Tucson) northeast to the New Mexico border through Duncan and south to the Mexico border through Bisbee

Heyder Pincushion
cream-to-pink flowers

MacDougal Pincushion
(pg. 27)
yellow flowers

MacDougal Pincushion
(pg. 27)
radial spines form a full circle

Compare: Heyder looks like MacDougal Pincushion (pg. 27) when not in bloom, but is easily identified when it is flowering. Heyder has cream-to-pink flowers, unlike the yellow flowers of MacDougal. MacDougal has a full circle of radial spines, whereas Heyder has a semicircle of radial spines.

Notes: A low, flat cactus with a stem that shrinks in winter to just above ground level or sometimes below. Grows among grasses or hides under shrubs and is often overlooked until it blooms. Some cactus lovers searching for a glimpse of this interesting plant have nearly walked on it while trying to find it. Ripe fruit, often present with the pale flowers, is the product of blooms from the previous year.

Both Heyder and MacDougal Pincushions are also called Cream Pincushion, being the only Arizona cacti that have a milky sap. Pincushions with this latex are sold in the drug stalls of Mexico and used as folk remedies. Tarahumara Natives of Mexico used this sap for headaches, ear problems, and more.

Uncommon in Arizona. Also found in southern New Mexico, Texas, southwestern Oklahoma, and northeastern Mexico. Easily seen in Tombstone's historic Boot Hill Cemetery, the final resting place of outlaws killed in the famous gunfight at the O.K. Corral. Cold hardy and frequently cultivated, this is one of the easiest (and slowest) pincushion cacti to grow.

spines

flower

MacDougal Pincushion
Mammillaria macdougalii

Size: H 1–3" (2.5–7.5 cm); W 3½–12" (9–30 cm)

Shape: low-growing, disk-shaped cactus with a depressed or flat top

Stem: single stem covered with conical green bumps (tubercles), each topped with a cluster of spines; stem has a milky white sap

Spines: white or pale yellow with dark reddish brown tips, ½–¾" (1–2 cm) long

Spine Clusters: 11–14 spines per cluster; each cluster often has 2 (sometimes 1) rigid central spines within a full circle of longer, needle-like radial spines pressed flat against the stem

Flower: yellow or greenish yellow blossoms form a wreath on the top of stem; each flower, 1–1½" (2.5–4 cm) wide, has slender petals with a pinkish brown stripe, and a yellow and green center

Blooming: April–May

Fruit: club-shaped, green-to-pink pod marked with pinkish purple, ⅝–1" (1.5–2.5 cm) long, with fleshy walls and tiny orange seeds

Zone/Habitat: higher desert scrub, grasslands, oak woodlands and interior chaparral from 3,600–5,900' (1,100–1,800 m); rocky hills and ridges, among grasses and agave plants, beneath oaks

Range: southeastern Arizona, from north of Tucson southeast through Sierra Vista to the Mexico border and west to Sasabe; seen in the lower elevations of mountains near Tucson and Nogales

MacDougal Pincushion
radial spines form a full
circle

Heyder Pincushion *(pg. 23)*
radial spines form a
semicircle

Heyder Pincushion *(pg. 23)*
usually a single dark-
tipped central spine

Compare: MacDougal has a full circle of radial spines, unlike Heyder Pincushion (pg. 23), which has a half circle of radial spines. Heyder often has only one dark-tipped central spine in each cluster; MacDougal usually has two central spines.

Notes: Also called Cream Pincushion for its milky sap, this broad, flat cactus is usually shorter than 3 inches (7.5 cm), but can reach a height of 20 inches (50 cm) when growing in the shade. It has the widest diameter of any pincushion in Arizona, but is often covered with grasses and not easily spotted. Following rain, the stem expands upward and is more noticeable.

The pale yellow flowers open in April and May. Light pink pods develop and ripen by fall or the next spring, but are seldom seen since birds and small mammals love to eat the fruit.

Found only in the lower elevations of mountains near Tucson and Nogales in Arizona, and in Sonora, Mexico. Can be seen with a little effort by driving up Reddington Pass Road (east of Tucson between the Santa Catalina and Rincon Mountains) until reaching grassland with scattered evergreen oaks. Search under the oaks and grass clumps to find it. Also can be seen in Molino Basin Campground, north of Tucson in the Santa Catalina Mountains.

spines

flower

Thornber Fishhook Pincushion
Mammillaria thornberi

Size: H 2–4" (5–10 cm)

Shape: dense clumps of 1–50 relatively short cylindrical green stems

Stem: multiple soft, slender stems; each stem, ¾–1⅜" (2–3.5 cm) wide and tapering at the base, is covered with cone-shaped bumps (tubercles) topped with clusters of spines

Spines: white or pale yellow with reddish brown or black tips, ⅕–⁷⁄₁₀" (.5–1.8 cm) long

Spine Clusters: slightly overlapping open clusters; each cluster has 14–22 spines with 1 long, hooked central spine pointing outward, surrounded by stiff, bristle-like radial spines

Flower: light pink blossoms in a ring near the top of stem; each star-shaped flower, ⅝–1¼" (1.5–3 cm) wide, has pointed petals with darker pink bases and midstripes around orange male flower parts (anthers) and magenta female flower parts (stigmas); blooms open 1–2 at a time

Blooming: April–May and July–August; after heavy rains

Fruit: club-shaped red pod, ³⁄₁₀–⅝" (.7–1.5 cm) long, edible, with fleshy walls and tiny black seeds; fruit appears nearly as often as the plant flowers, ripening 3–6 months after blooming

Zone/Habitat: desert scrub between 1,100–2,000' (335–610 m); valleys, along washes, flats, deep soils

Range: south central Arizona, including the Tohono O'odham and San Xavier Indian Reservations

Thornber Fishhook Pincushion
slimmer, more numerous stems

Arizona Fishhook Pincushion *(pg. 39)*
fatter, rounder stems

Arizona Fishhook Pincushion *(pg. 39)*
spines cover green stems

Compare: Very similar to Arizona Fishhook Pincushion (pg. 39), which is more abundant and widespread. Thornber has larger clumps of slimmer and more numerous stems and its spines do not cover the green color of the tubercles, as they often do in Arizona Fishhook.

Notes: Also called Thornber Nipple Cactus. Pincushion cacti are covered with bumps (tubercles), giving the genus its Latin name *Mammillaria* or "nipple." Can be confused with a small hedgehog cactus. Pincushions differ from hedgehogs by the arrangement of tubercles in spirals (one clockwise, one counterclockwise) around stems, unlike the vertical ribs of hedgehogs. In addition, while many pincushion species have hooked central spines, no hedgehog does.

Limited population size as well as man-made and natural stresses threaten the continued existence of this cactus. Once grew in the millions in the Avra Valley west of Tucson, where after a hard freeze in 1937, few plants remained. Almost always grows beneath a desert shrub or tree that shields it from cold and heat. Sometimes among fallen spiny stems underneath Jumping Cholla (pg. 203), which protect seedlings from animals looking for food. Dedicated volunteers from the Tucson Cactus & Succulent Society, Inc. (TCSS) rescue cacti from areas threatened by development, digging individual plants laboriously by hand. This is one of the rarer plants that TCSS has worked hard to preserve.

spines

flower

fruit

Corkyseed Fishhook Pincushion
Mammillaria tetrancistra

Size: H 2–6" (5–15 cm)

Shape: dense clumps of 1–9 (sometimes as many as 30) short cylindrical stems

Stem: single or multiple soft stems, each 1⅜–2¾" (3.5–7 cm) wide, covered with cone-shaped bumps (tubercles) that wind around the stem in spirals (1 clockwise, 1 counterclockwise), but which are mostly hidden by the spine clusters

Spines: dark brown or white with dark tips, ¼–1" (.6–2.5 cm) long

Spine Clusters: dense interlacing clusters; each cluster has 21–64 spines with 3–4 hooked dark central spines surrounded by 2 layers of bristle-like white radial spines

Flower: dark pink blossoms form a wreath near the top of stems; each flower, 1–1⅜" (2.5–3.5 cm) wide, has petals with lighter pink edges and a center of yellow to yellow-green

Blooming: April and after heavy monsoon rains in July

Fruit: club-shaped red pod, ⅝–1¼" (1.5–3 cm) long, smooth, fleshy, edible, containing numerous pitted black seeds with tan cork-like appendages

seeds

Zone/Habitat: desert scrub up to 3,000' (915 m); gravelly canyon floors, rocky hillsides, ridges, often among creosote bushes

Range: southwestern Arizona and northward to extreme western areas of the state near the Colorado River and north of Lake Mead

Corkyseed Fishhook Pincushion
3–4 hooked central spines

Arizona Fishhook Pincushion *(pg. 39)*
usually only a single hooked central spine

Arizona Fishhook Pincushion *(pg. 39)*
fewer radial spines make a neat, tidy stem

Compare: Most similar to Arizona Fishhook Pincushion (pg. 39), which overlaps its range in the southwestern part of the state, but Arizona Fishhook has neat radial spines, firm stems and a single hooked central spine, unlike the unkempt radial spines, soft stems, and 3–4 hooked central spines of Corkyseed.

Notes: Commonly called Corkyseed Pincushion for the cork-like appendages on its small black seeds. A hardy cactus, abundant and widespread in the harsh and dry Sonoran and Mojave Deserts of western Arizona. Sometimes intermingles with Arizona Fishhook Pincushion beneath desert shrubs and trees. Field identification can be done with a stick and a mild poke to see if the stem is soft (Corkyseed) or firm (Arizona).

Corkyseed flower buds produced during the preceding summer remain dormant throughout the winter. About a week after the first summer rain, the showy blossoms open and appear too large for the plant. After the flowers are pollinated by bees, fruit forms and ripens over the next six months, a few at a time. The red pods do not last long as they are quickly picked off by birds, small rodents, and people.

spines

flower

fruit

Arizona Fishhook Pincushion
Mammillaria grahamii

Size: H 3–6½" (7.5–16 cm)

Shape: dense clumps of 1–9 (can have as many as 30) cylindrical or round stems

Stem: multiple stiff stems, each 1½–2¾" (4–7 cm) wide, covered with conical bumps (tubercles) that wind around the stem in spirals, but which are partially hidden by the spine clusters

Spines: mostly white or gray, ¼–1" (.6–2.5 cm) long

Spine Clusters: overlapping clusters; each cluster has 1–3 reddish brown-to-black central spines (only 1 is hooked), surrounded by 18–28 bristle-like spines pressed flat against the stem

Flower: star-shaped pink blossoms form a wreath near the top of stems; each flower, 1" (2.5 cm) wide, has petals with dark pink stripes and bases surrounding a center of orange male flower parts (anthers) and green female flower parts (stigmas)

Blooming: April–September; about 7–8 days after heavy rainfall; each plant can bloom several times during the summer

Fruit: club-shaped, scarlet red pod, ½–1¼" (1–3 cm) long, is smooth, fleshy, edible, and contains small black seeds

densely spiny

Zone/Habitat: desert scrub, grasslands, oak woodlands, interior chaparral up to 4,600' (1,400 m); beneath shrubs, trees or other cacti, hills, canyons, slopes, flats

Range: most of the southern half of Arizona, ranging farther north in the western part of the state, from Needles on the California border to the border with Mexico and southeast through Phoenix and Tucson to the southeastern corner of Arizona

Arizona Fishhook Pincushion
green stigmas

Thornber Fishhook Pincushion *(pg. 31)*
magenta stigmas

Corkyseed Fishhook Pincushion *(pg. 35)*
stouter, more numerous radial spines

Compare: Similar to Thornber Fishhook Pincushion (pg. 31), but Thornber clumps have numerous, slimmer stems with less dense spines that reveal the green color of the stems, in contrast to the fewer, fatter stems and dense spines of Arizona Fishhook. When these two cacti are in bloom, compare the stigma color of the flower. Also looks like Corkyseed Fishhook Pincushion (pg. 35), but Corkyseed has stouter, unkempt radial spines and soft stems.

Notes: Although the most abundant and widespread pincushion cactus in southern Arizona, this small cactus is often overlooked because it usually grows beneath desert shrubs and trees. These "nurse" plants provide shelter against sun or frost and protect the cactus from being trampled. In winter, when stems lose water and shrivel, the pincushion is even less noticeable. Gray spines cover the stems, making the plant look more like a rock at first glance. Spines don't entirely cover the green stems when they swell with summer rainwater. As the pink flowers or red fruit emerge in a ring at the top, the short clumps suddenly become conspicuous.

The longest slender brown central spine in each spine cluster rises above the network of gray radial spines, especially on top of the stem, making the cactus look like a gray pincushion stuck with pins. The thin "pins" are hooked at the tips, giving rise to "Fishhook" in the common name. Also called Graham's Nipple Cactus for its conical knobs (tubercles), resembling nipples.

spines

flower

fruit

Smallflower Fishhook Cactus
Sclerocactus parviflorus

Size: H 2–18" (5–45 cm); W 1–6" (3–15 cm)

Shape: low growing round or cylindrical cactus

Stem: green, usually single stem, infrequently multiple stems, with 10–16 rows of ribs with prominent bumps (tubercles), each tipped with a cluster of variable length, hooked and straight spines that often obscure the color of the stem

Spines: white, straw-colored, brown, purplish pink, to black ⅓–3" (1–9 cm) long

Spine Clusters: shaggy overlapping clusters: each cluster has 4–8 central spines surrounded by 8–17 radial spines; 1–5 of the central spines at top of plant are purplish black and hooked; central spines on sides of plant are mostly white and straighter

Flower: cup-shaped, often rose to light pink, yellow, or rarely white blossoms form a dense tuft at the top of stem: each pleasantly scented flower, ¾–2" (2–5 cm) wide, has yellow, green, or purple flowers parts in the center

Blooming: April–May

Fruit: cylindrical pod, ½–1" (1–3 cm) long, green maturing to light pink, retains dried flowers parts at tip, splitting open irregularly to release tiny, black seeds

immature plant

Zone/Habitat: Pinyon-juniper woods, desert grasslands, among saltbush or other low brush communities between 3,000–7,000' (910–2,130 m) on hills, arroyos, canyons, tablelands.

Range: sporadic in the northern third of Arizona

Smallflower Fishhook Cactus
some central spines are hooked

Johnson Pineapple Cactus *(pg. 63)*
lacks hooked central spines

Johnson Pineapple Cactus *(pg. 63)*
red spines make the plant appear pink

Compare: Superficially looks like the distantly related, red-spined Johnson Pineapple Cactus. Johnson Pineapple Cactus lacks hooked central spines and is found only in western Arizona.

Notes: Smallflower Fishhook grows larger, is the most widespread, and the most common cactus in its genus. Found in northern Arizona, northwestern New Mexico, southwestern Colorado, and the eastern half of Utah. It is one of the best known cacti of cold American deserts as it can tolerate temperature below zero degrees Fahrenheit (-20 °C). Rarely cultivated as it needs perfect drainage or it dies from root rot. Its appearance in flower color, number, and color of spines, as well as other characteristics varies greatly between localities. While sometimes tiny and half-buried in the soil, stems are usually 4–7 inches tall, but relatively giant specimens occur and can be up to 1½ feet (.5m) high. Due to this variability in appearance, botanists still disagree about its classification, but four subspecies are currently recognized. Common and can be seen along the nature trail in Pipe Springs National Monument.

tubercle groove

flower

fruit

Robust-spine Beehive Cactus

Coryphantha robustispina

Size: H 2–6" (5–15 cm); W 2–3½" (5–9 cm)

Shape: low-growing round or beehive-shaped cactus

Stem: single stem covered with large thick conical bumps (tubercles), each with an obvious groove on the upper surface and tipped with a spine cluster

Spines: yellow, gray, or brown, ½–1⅜" (1–3.5 cm) long

Spine Clusters: 1–4 stout, hooked, or curved central spines surrounded by 6–16 shorter radial spines forming a full circle around the center of the cluster

Flower: frilly, pale yellow flowers in a dense cluster at the top of stem; each blossom, 2–2½" (5–6 cm) wide, has long slender petals around a yellow center; bloom held partially closed by the spines

Blooming: April–September; 5 days following the first warm summer rain; flowers last only 1 day

Fruit: cone-shaped juicy green pod, 1½–2" (4–5 cm) long, remaining green when ripe, obscured by spines and often mistaken for a tubercle

Zone/Habitat: desert scrub, grasslands and oak/pinyon pine/juniper woodlands from 3,000–5,900' (915–1,800 m); bajadas, grassy hills, valleys, open areas, among creosote bushes, saltbushes, or grasses

Range: parts of the southeastern quarter of Arizona, from south of Tucson to Nogales on the Mexico border, and around San Simon and Portal near the border with New Mexico

**Robust-spine Beehive
Cactus**
cone-shaped tubercles
and smooth spines

Emory Barrel (pg. 103)
stem has vertical folds
and grooves

Emory Barrel (pg. 103)
central spine has ridges
and a flattened tip

Compare: Robust-spine Beehive Cactus has stouter spines than other beehive cacti, looking almost like a tiny barrel cactus with hooked central spines. Emory Barrel (pg. 103) and other barrel cacti have vertical folds in the stem (ribs) and usually flattened central spines with horizontal ridges, unlike the separate cone-shaped tubercles and smooth needle-shaped spines of the Robust-spine.

Notes: Found only in Arizona, southern New Mexico, western Texas, and northern Mexico. Listed as endangered under the Endangered Species Act. In many areas the plants are low in density, with only 1–2 plants per 4 acres (1.6 ha). This cactus is becoming even rarer due to loss of habitat from development in the Altar and Santa Cruz Valleys.

Species name *robustispina* is for its stout rigid spines. Also called Devil's Pincushion for the spines. The thick, cone-shaped bumps (tubercles) that show through the spines resemble the skin of a pineapple. Called by another name, Pima Pineapple Cactus, for this resemblance and for the main county in which it grows.

The slightest rain (less than a quarter inch) triggers blooming five days later, even while other plants nearby remain dehydrated. Its pale yellow flowers cannot always open fully because the spines get in the way. Cone-shaped fruit forms several months after flowering and stays green, looking like additional tubercles.

spines

flower

Spinystar
Escobaria vivipara

Size: H 1–8" (2.5–20 cm); W 1–4½" (2.5–11 cm)

Shape: low-growing round or cylindrical cactus with a flat top; in winter, becomes more flat-topped and may be over halfway underground

Stem: 1–24 green stems, each covered with spirals of large conical bumps (tubercles) grooved on upper surface and tipped with overlapping spines that obscure the stem color

Spines: white or pinkish gray with dark reddish brown tips, ³⁄₁₀–1" (.7–2.5 cm) long

Spine Clusters: 3–14 rigid central spines that point outward, upward and downward, and a circle of 10–40 stiff, needle-like radial spines around the center, pressed closely against the stem

Flower: frilly pink flowers in dense bouquet at the top of stem; each bloom, 1–2½" (2.5–6 cm) wide, has orange-yellow male flower parts (anthers) and white female flower parts (stigmas)

Blooming: April–August; 6 days after the first summer rain

Fruit: juicy green pod, ½–1" (1–2.5 cm) long, remaining green but tinged with purplish marks when ripe, containing reddish brown, pitted seeds

immature mound

Zone/Habitat: all life zones from 3,000–8,900' (915–2,710 m); low hills, mountaintops, open areas, among grasses or pines, under bushes

Range: eastern two-thirds of Arizona, ranging from the border with Utah south to Mexico; includes the area from just west of Nogales to east of Tucson and Phoenix, then northwest through Wickenburg to the Nevada border

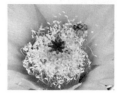

Spinystar
tubercles not in vertical rows

Needle-spine Pineapple Cactus *(pg. 59)*
tubercles in vertical rows

Needle-spine Pineapple Cactus *(pg. 59)*
red, not white, stigmas

Compare: Needle-spine Pineapple Cactus (pg. 59) has tubercles in vertical rows, unlike the tubercle spirals of Common Beehive. When young, Common Beehive can be easily mistaken for Needle-spine, but Needle-spine lacks a groove on the upper side of its tubercles that the mature Common Beehive has.

Notes: The most widespread and abundant cactus in its genus which was named after the Mexican naturalists Romulo and Numo Escobar. Species name, *vivipara* is Latin for "sprouting from the parent plant", referring to the production of new buds on old stems that drop off and can become new plants.

Spinystar resembles pincushions, differing from them by flower position and tubercle grooves. Named for its spiny appearance; however immature plants lack the longer, outward-pointing central spines of the mature plants, having only white radial spines.

Previously lumped in with the beehive cacti in the genus *Coryphantha*, Spinystar was then called Common Beehive Cactus for its abundance and wide range. Ranges from Canada to northern Mexico, as far west as Nevada and as far east as Oklahoma. May bloom at different times across its range in Arizona, due to the patchy distribution of summer rains. Fruit forms and ripens 2-5 months afterward. It is extremely cold hardy to -8 °F (-22 °C) and is one of only four cacti species that grows in Canada.

spines

flower

immature fruit

Woven-spine Pineapple Cactus
Echinomastus intertextus

PINEAPPLE
BEEHIVE

Size: H 2–7" (5–18 cm); W 1–4" (2.5–10 cm)

Shape: low-growing round or cylindrical cactus

Stem: single dull green stem with 11–13 wide vertical ribs lined with spine clusters; ribs twist around the stem as the cactus elongates with age

Spines: white to pink to dull gray, ⅕–¾" (.5–2 cm) long

Spine Clusters: interlacing, spider-like clusters; each cluster has 1–2 long central spines pointing upward and 1 shorter, outward-pointing central spine surrounded by 13–25 stiff, slightly inward-curving radial spines pressed closely against the stem

Flower: 3–5 coconut-scented, pale pink flowers in a dense cluster at the top of stem; each blossom, 1–1⅜" (2.5–3.5 cm) wide, has brown midstripes on outside of petals and a center of yellow male flower parts (anthers) and yellow or pink female flower parts (stigmas)

Blooming: February–April

Fruit: round green pod, ⅝" (1.5 cm) long, drying to tan when mature and releasing seeds through a pore at the base

immature cactus

wide ribs

Zone/Habitat: desert scrub and grasslands, occasionally with some oaks or junipers, between 3,500–6,000' (1,065–1,830 m); ridges, grassy slopes, bajadas, hidden under shrubs or grasses, often among volcanic rocks

Range: southeastern corner of Arizona, from just north of Wilcox south to Douglas and from Patagonia east to the New Mexico border

**Needle-spine Pineapple
Cactus** *(pg. 59)*
thinner ribs and pink
radial spines

**Johnson Pineapple
Cactus** *(pg. 63)*
dense red spines

Spinystar *(pg. 51)*
resembles immature
Woven-spine plants

Compare: Much like Needle-spine Pineapple Cactus (pg. 59), but Needle-spine has thinner ribs and pink radial spines, not white. Needle-spine range overlaps with Woven-spine only in southeastern Arizona. Johnson Pineapple Cactus (pg. 63) has dull red spines. Young Woven-spine cacti can look like Spinystar (pg. 51).

Notes: A small single-stemmed cactus, easily overlooked since it is often hidden by grasses. Young stems are flat-topped and round, growing more cylindrical with age. Radial spines are white. Central spines are pink to dull gray. Sometimes called White-spine Fishhook Cactus, although it lacks hooked spines. The inward-curving radial and the central spines, which are almost all pressed against the stem, make it appear as if the cactus can be handled with bare hands without being stuck

One of the earliest flowering cacti in Arizona, sometimes blooming in February, but more commonly in March and April. Creamy white-to-pale pink flowers are large and showy, with pale yellow and pink flower parts (anthers and stigmas) in the centers. Fruit develops in April through June, turning dry and tan.

Grows as a single cactus or scattered in colonies in Arizona, New Mexico, Texas, and the Mexican states of Chihuahua and Sonora. Sometimes called Chihuahuan Pineapple Cactus.

57

spines

flower

immature fruit

Needle-spine Pineapple Cactus
Echinomastus erectocentrus

Size: H 3–9" (7.5–23 cm); W 1½–4" (4–10 cm)

Shape: low-growing round or pineapple-shaped cactus

Stem: single green stem, sometimes multiple stems, with 18–21 narrow vertical ribs with prominent bumps (tubercles), each tipped with spine clusters that obscure much of the stem color

Spines: purplish pink to white with dark tips, ½–¾" (1–2 cm) long

Spine Clusters: interlacing clusters; each cluster has 1–3 longer, upward-pointing central spines and 12–18 stiff radial spines pressed closely against the stem; immature cacti lack central spines

Flower: pale or rosy pink flowers in a dense tuft at the top of stem; each blossom, 1½–2½" (4–6 cm) wide, has slender petals surrounding yellow male flower parts (anthers) and red female flower parts (stigmas)

Blooming: March–April

Fruit: cylindrical green pod, ¾" (2 cm) long, drying to tan when mature and releasing black seeds through 1 vertical slit

red stigmas

Zone/Habitat: desert scrub and grasslands between 1,200–6,000' (365–1,830 m); slopes, bajadas, in open areas or among shrubs or grasses, volcanic or granite rock, in light-colored gravelly soil with limestone

Range: scattered areas in southern Arizona, from Lukeville on the Mexico border north through Ajo, from Mammoth south through Benson almost to Fairbank, and the area just northeast of Florence

Woven-spine Pineapple Cactus *(pg. 55)*
green stem is visible

Spinystar *(pg. 51)*
light-colored stigmas

Spinystar *(pg. 51)*
immature plants resemble young Needle-spine

Compare: Woven-spine Pineapple Cactus (pg. 55) spine clusters are whiter, farther apart, and do not hide the green color of the stem. Needle-spine has red female flower parts (stigmas); Spinystar (pg. 51) stigmas are greenish white. Young Needle-spine and young Common Beehive plants can lack central spines, but Needle-spine tubercles are in vertical rows, unlike the evenly spaced tubercles of Common Beehive.

Notes: A small, pretty cactus, usually with one stem. Sometimes forms small clumps of several stems, appearing reddish on top. The red color comes from the upward-pointing maroon central spines, which are more conspicuous on the upper stem. The stems are hidden among tall grasses during the summer monsoons, but are more noticeable at other times when the ground is almost bare. Its showy flowers, pinkish white to darker pink, open in spring and are pollinated by ten species of native wild bees.

Rare, restricted to Arizona and Sonora, Mexico. In Pima County, human population growth has slowed from an incredible 25–93% increase each decade in the last century to less than 9% growth from 2010–2022. Development is a still a significant threat and the possibility of extinction of this cactus is very high. A variety of this species, called Acuna Cactus is listed as endangered already.

spines

flower

Johnson Pineapple Cactus
Echinomastus johnsonii

Size: H 4–10" (10–25 cm); W 3–6" (7.5–15 cm)

Shape: low-growing round or pineapple-shaped cactus

Stem: single green stem with 18–21 narrow vertical ribs with prominent bumps (tubercles), each tipped with spines that partially cover the stem color

Spines: red to grayish lavender, ¼–1½" (.6–4 cm) long

Spine Clusters: dense interlacing clusters; each cluster has 13–24 similar-looking central and radial spines with spreading, slightly curved central spines and radial spines that are longest at the sides of the cluster

Flower: funnel-shaped, magenta or yellow blossoms in a dense tuft atop the stem; each flower, 1½–2½" (4–6 cm) wide, has blunt-tipped petals with maroon bases and a center of yellow and white or green

Blooming: March–May

Fruit: round to oval green pod, ½" (1 cm) long, drying to tan when mature and releasing black seeds through a vertical slit

Zone/Habitat: desert scrub from 1,500–4,600' (460–1,400 m); rocky hillsides, bajadas, granite or limestone soils

Range: far northwestern edge of Arizona along the border with California and Nevada

Johnson Pineapple Cactus
like young barrel cacti, but no hooked central spines

Compass Barrel *(pg. 111)*
hooked central spines and white bristle-like radial spines

Needle-spine Pineapple Cactus *(pg. 59)*
shorter and fewer central spines

Compare: Compass Barrel (pg. 111) has hooked central spines. While the range of Needle-spine Pineapple Cactus (pg. 59) does not overlap with Johnson Pineapple Cactus, they are very much alike. Needle-spine has shorter and fewer central spines, making it appear less spiny. Needle-spine flower petals are slender and pointed, unlike the blunt-tipped petals of Johnson.

Notes: At maturity, about the size and shape of a pineapple. This single-stemmed, densely spiny cactus is larger than the other pineapple cacti in Arizona. The long, dull reddish spines make the cactus appear pink from a distance and are all similar, with not much difference between radial and central spines.

Western Arizona populations of Johnson Pineapple Cacti have yellow flowers with brown throats. At lower elevations of the Mojave Desert, such as in Death Valley, Johnson flowers are magenta with maroon throats. Unlike other Arizona pineapple cacti, Johnson has wider flower petals with rounded edges, not pointed tips.

Sometimes called Mojave Pineapple Cactus for the desert where it grows. Seen in Hummingbird Springs Wilderness, a 31,200–acre (12,480 ha) preserve west of Phoenix. Mostly found in Arizona, but also in southern Nevada, southwestern Utah, and southeastern California in the area of Death Valley.

spines

flower

Santa Cruz Beehive Cactus
Coryphantha recurvata

Size: H 4–10" (10–25 cm)

Shape: mounds, 12–36" (30–91 cm) wide, of 1–50 round or beehive-shaped stems with flat tops

Stem: single or multiple green stems, each 4–6" (10–15 cm) wide, covered with small conical bumps (tubercles) with a groove on the upper surface and tipped with delicate spines that cover the stem color

Spines: yellow, tan, or gray with dark red tips, ½–¾" (1–2 cm) long

Spine Clusters: dense clusters in a crosshatched pattern; each cluster has 1–2 longer central spines pointing outward and curving downward and 6–16 stiff, inward-curving radial spines forming a full circle around the center of the cluster

Flower: lemon yellow or greenish yellow flowers rim the top of stem, forming a wreath; each blossom, 1–1½" (2.5–4 cm) wide, has long slender pointed petals around yellow and green flower parts

Blooming: June–July

Fruit: oval, sparsely pulpy, greenish white pod, ½" (1 cm) long, drying to bronze-tinged yellowish green when mature; pods form and ripen in winter from November through January, months after flowering

Zone/Habitat: grasslands and oak woodlands between 4,000–6,000' (1,220–1,830 m); rocky slopes and hillsides with good grass cover, rock crevices, among grasses, underneath oaks, in valleys, mesas

Range: small area in southeastern Arizona, from Tubac south to Nogales on the Mexico border in the Parajito, Atascosa, and Tumacacori Mountains

Santa Cruz Beehive Cactus
tubercles not in vertical rows

Needle-spine Pineapple Cactus *(pg. 59)*
tubercles in vertical rows

Spinystar *(pg. 51)*
straight central spines

Compare: Needle-spine Pineapple Cactus (pg. 59) has vertical rows of tubercles that bear spines. Spinystar (pg. 51) has straight central spines at maturity, unlike the down-curving central spines of Santa Cruz.

Notes: The largest cactus of its genus in Arizona. Like all species in *Coryphantha*, this one has a groove on the upper surface of its tubercles. Stems are globe-shaped with a flat top (resembling a beehive, thus the common name) and neat in appearance due to the short radial spines that curve slightly back against the stem and the downward-curving central spine. Spines give it the species name *recurvata*, meaning "curved backward" in Latin.

Forms large mounds of densely packed stems that glisten like gold from the yellow spines. Most beehive cacti bloom in tufts at the top of stems, but like pincushion cacti, this beehive species produces yellow flowers in rings near the top of stems. These add to the overall golden color when in bloom.

Limited in distribution in the United States to scattered populations in Arizona's Santa Cruz County, after which it was named. Can be seen near the Mexico border in Sycamore Canyon, a unique canyon with a year-round stream accessible only by a rough dirt road and then by foot. More widespread in Sonora, Mexico. While cactus collecting is illegal in Arizona, more accessible colonies of this species are disappearing due to collectors.

spines

flower

fruit

Fendler Hedgehog
Echinocereus fendleri

Size: H 3–7" (7.5–18 cm)

Shape: loose clusters of 1–20 cylindrical stems

Stem: multiple upright or reclining, semisoft stems, each 1½–3" (4–7.5 cm) wide, with 8–11 wavy ribs with stout, sparse spines

Spines: black or brown or white to gray with a dark stripe beneath, ½–1½" (1–4 cm) long

Spine Clusters: clusters line each rib; each cluster has 1 (sometimes 2–3) longer, dark-tipped, outward-pointing central spine surrounded by 4–10 short, stout radial spines pressed against the stem, with the longest radial stem pointing downward

Flower: 1 to several funnel-shaped, brilliant pink blooms on the sides of stems near the top; each large flower, 2–4½" (5–11 cm) wide, has layers of petals with darker bases and midstripes and a center of pale yellow and green

Blooming: April–May

Fruit: spiny oval red pod, ¾–1¼" (2–3 cm) long, drops most of its spines when ripe, with magenta-to-red pulp containing many small black seeds

Zone/Habitat: grasslands, oak/pinyon pine/juniper woodlands and interior chaparral between 3,900–6,800' (1,190–2,075 m); south-facing slopes, mesquite woodlands (bosques), bajadas, ridges, limestone or volcanic rocky soils

Range: northeastern quarter of Arizona, from Flagstaff north to Grand Canyon Village and southeast to south of Payson, ranging east to the border of New Mexico and south along the border; most of the southeastern corner of the state; also a small area around Cottonwood, north of Prescott

Fendler Hedgehog
dark brown stripe on
radial spines

Pink-flowered Hedgehog
(pg. 91)
no stripe on radial
spines

Bonker Hedgehog
(pg. 75)
more ribs and
shorter spines

Compare: Resembles Pink-flowered Hedgehog (pg. 91), which has longer central spines and radial spines that lack a dark brown stripe beneath. Bonker Hedgehog (pg. 75) is also similar, but its fruit has pinkish white pulp, spines are shorter and stems have more and narrower ribs.

Notes: Fendler Hedgehog occurs in the wild as a solitary plant or grows in clumps and forms extensive colonies. A wide-ranging cactus found in Arizona, southeastern Colorado, western Texas, most of New Mexico, and northern Mexico. Growing at higher elevations, this small plant has fewer spines and is shorter than most hedgehog species in Arizona. Immature Fendler cacti have flattened, all-white spines and don't resemble mature plants.

Frequently cultivated for its big, bright pink flowers, growing to maturity and blooming about five years after seeds are planted. After flowering in spring, the red pods ripen from June through August. The edible sweet fruit does not stay on the cactus long since it is quickly eaten by birds and small mammals.

spines

flower

fruit

Bonker Hedgehog
Echinocereus bonkerae

Size: H 5–8" (8–20 cm)

Shape: loose clumps of 5–15 short cylindrical stems

Stem: multiple upright, light green stems, each 1½–3" (4–7.5 cm) wide, with 12–18 vertical ribs with short spines

Spines: pinkish brown or white to gray with pink bases and brown tips, ⅕–¼" (.5–.6 cm) long

Spine Clusters: straight rigid spines in clusters, spaced ⅓–¾" (.8–2 cm) apart on ribs; each cluster with 1–2 dark-tipped central spines pointing outward and a semicircle of 11–14 radial spines pressed against the stem

Flower: 1 to several trumpet-shaped, bright magenta-to-dark purple flowers on the upper sides of stems; each bloom, 2–4" (5–10 cm) wide, has overlapping petals with greenish purple bases surrounding yellow and green flower parts

Blooming: April

Fruit: spiny, round, orange-red pod, ⅝–1" (1.5–2.5 cm) long, with spines that are easy to brush off; fleshy and edible pinkish white pulp contains many small black seeds and tastes like strawberry

Zone/Habitat: grasslands and oak woodlands up to 6,500' (1,980 m); flats, hills, canyons, bajadas

Range: central to southern Arizona, from the north side of the Santa Catalina Mountains (north of Tucson), ranging north through Mammoth, Winkelman, and Globe and northwest to Payson

Pink-flowered Hedgehog
(pg. 91)
pink flowers

Pink-flowered Hedgehog
(pg. 91)
longer spines obscure
the stem

Fendler Hedgehog *(pg. 71)*
fewer ribs, longer spines

Compare: Resembles Pink-flowered Hedgehog (pg. 91), which has lighter-colored flowers and 1–4 central spines that are longer than the short spines of Bonker. Unlike Bonker, spines of Pink-flowered make its green stem difficult to see. Fendler Hedgehog (pg. 71) is similar, but its fruit has red pulp and stems have fewer ribs and stouter spines.

Notes: Found only in Arizona. The green stems of this cactus are fully exposed to the sun, showing clearly through its short spines. Chlorophyll in the cells of its green skin use the sun's energy to power the photosynthesis of nutrients without using moisture-expending leaves. Dwarfing this plant are its eye-catching flowers, which are pollinated by medium-sized bees.

Like the other hedgehogs, ribs enable this cactus to store water, expanding like accordion pleats. In addition, the waxy skin, lack of leaves, and shade from spines slows water loss due to evaporation. Its expansive root system absorbs water fast during the rainy season, and the outer roots die back when rains are over.

Once thought to be a short-spined variety of Fendler Hedgehog or Pink-flowered Hedgehog, but now considered a separate species. The pattern and length of spines in the spine clusters must be closely inspected to differentiate Bonker from these two species.

spines

flower

fruit

Arizona Rainbow Hedgehog
Echinocereus rigidissimus

Size: H 3–12" (7.5–30 cm), but more often 3–6" (7.5–15 cm); W 3½–4½" (9–11 cm)

Shape: low-growing stout cylindrical cactus

Stem: single green stem with 18–23 vertical ribs with a lattice of closely spaced spines forming alternating horizontal bands of pink, white, yellow, or brown that mostly cover the stem color

Spines: pink or pink and white, ¼–½" (.6–1 cm) long

Spine Clusters: overlapping comb-like clusters; each cluster lacks central spines, but has 15–23 short, stiff radial spines pressed tightly against the stem

Flower: several bowl-shaped, brilliant pink blooms on the upper sides of the stem; each flower, 2½–3½" (6–9 cm) wide, has overlapping petals with white or yellow bases around an orange, yellow, and green center; unopened flower buds are extremely spiny and appear fuzzy

Blooming: May–July; over a period of several weeks

Fruit: spiny, round, green or purple pod, 1–2" (2.5–5 cm) long, containing white pulp with many small black seeds; pod ripens almost 3 months after flowering

flower buds

Zone/Habitat: grasslands, oak woodlands, and interior chaparral from 4,000–5,500' (1,220–1,675 m); rocky hills, steep canyons

Range: southeastern corner of Arizona, from along the Mexico border north on both sides of Interstate 19 almost to Tubac and east to the New Mexico border through Benson and Wilcox

Arizona Rainbow Hedgehog
lacks central spines

Bonker Hedgehog *(pg. 75)*
1–2 white or gray central spines

Woven-spine Pineapple Cactus *(pg. 55)*
1–3 short central spines

Compare: Arizona Rainbow Hedgehog plants lacking horizontal bands of pink color could be mistaken for the short-spined Bonker Hedgehog (pg. 75), but it has 1–2 central spines. May more likely be confused with the less closely related Woven-spine Pineapple Cactus (pg. 55), but it has 1–3 central spines.

Notes: Sometimes occurring in abundance on a hillside, this stout little hedgehog is a pretty sight with its pink and white spines, along with its big and showy pink flowers. "Rainbow" in the common name refers to the colored bands on the stem, each reflecting a year's growth. Some populations lack most of the pink color and the horizontal bands, appearing whitish green with white spines almost covering the green stem.

Arizona Rainbow does not have central spines. The species name *rigidissimus* refers to the stiffness of its radial spines. These spines overlap and are pressed so closely to the stem that people can handle the plant with bare hands and still not get pricked.

Found only in southeastern Arizona, southwestern New Mexico, and northern Mexico. Readily seen along West Ruby Road (south of Tucson) from Interstate 19 to Ruby and Arivaca. Can be cultivated, grown only from seed. Grows and blooms indoors with sufficient light. Prefers slightly acidic soil.

spines

flower

Nichol Hedgehog
Echinocereus nicholii

Size: H 8–12" (20–30 cm), some up to 18" (45 cm)

Shape: large loose clumps of 16–30 cylindrical stems

Stem: multiple upright green stems; each stem, 2½–3½" (6–9 cm) wide, with 10–13 vertical ribs with dense spines that mostly obscure the stem color

Spines: golden yellow, ⅕–3" (.5–7.5 cm) long

Spine Clusters: dense clusters of straight, needle-like spines; each cluster has 4–6 outward-pointing central spines (1 is white, flattened, and pointing downward) and 8–12 radial spines pointing outward

Flower: 1 to several pink flowers on the upper half of stems; each narrow, cup-shaped flower, 1½–2½" (4–6 cm) wide, has petals with darker pink mid-stripes around pale yellow and green flower parts

Blooming: March–April

Fruit: spiny oval green pod, turning bronze when ripe, 1–1½" (2.5–4 cm) long, edible, with very juicy white pulp containing many small black seeds; not easily detached from the stem, even when ripe

Zone/Habitat: desert scrub between 1,000–3,000' (305–915 m); open areas, flats, gravelly slopes, bajadas, granite rock outcrops

Range: small portion of southern Arizona, from Lukeville on the Mexico border north through Ajo and northeast almost to Marana

Nichol Hedgehog
golden yellow spines

Engelmann Hedgehog
(pg. 95)
multicolored spines

Engelmann Hedgehog
(pg. 95)
red fruit

Compare: Resembles Engelmann Hedgehog (pg. 95), which has multicolored spines and red fruit, not all-yellow spines and bronze fruit like Nichol Hedgehog.

Notes: This showy golden cactus with its pink flowers is a favorite of desert landscapers and is frequently seen in cities and towns throughout the Southwest. Also called Golden Hedgehog, with cultivated varieties sold under that name in nurseries. Its spines appear to glow from within when backlit by the sun.

Needs little water, but tolerates colder temperatures poorly. The spiny fruit has a juicy white pulp and is not easily detached from the stem when ripe. The Pima People ate the fruit pulp raw after carefully removing the spines.

In the wild, this species is found only in Arizona and Mexico. In the northern Mexican state of Sonora, near Guaymas, there is a subspecies that has crimson flowers. Nichol Hedgehog is most easily seen in the Silverbell Mountains of Ironwood Forest National Monument, a 129,000–acre (51,600 ha) preserve known for its numerous petroglyph or rock art sites. It is also common in Organ Pipe Cactus National Monument and Cabeza Prieta National Wildlife Refuge.

Kingcup

spines

flower

Kingcup Hedgehog
Echinocereus triglochidiatus

Scarlet Hedgehog
Echinocereus coccineus

Size: H 4–18" (10–45 cm)

Shape: loose cluster or dense mounds of 1–76 (sometimes up to 300) cylindrical or round stems

Stem: multiple upright, light green stems, each 2–5" (5–13 cm) wide, with 5–12 vertical ribs with spines; ribs sometimes have bumps (tubercles)

Spines: pale gray, yellow, brown, or black, turning gray with age, ⅝–5" (1.5–13 cm) long

Spine Clusters: each cluster has 1 outward-pointing central spine (may lack a central spine) and 1–10 radial spines pressed against the stem or pointing outward with the central spine; all spines are straight and look similar

Flower: 1 to several deep velvet red or red-orange flowers on the upper sides of stems; each cup-shaped bloom, 2–4" (5–10 cm) wide, has petals with light bases around pinkish purple male flower parts (anthers)

Blooming: April–June, depending on elevation; blooms stay open 24 hours a day for over a week

Fruit: round, spiny, green or pink pod, ¾–1⅜" (2–3.5 cm) long, has white pulp containing numerous small black seeds

Scarlet

Zone/Habitat: all life zones except lower desert scrub, from 3,000–9,000' (915–2,745 m); open areas or under trees, rocky hilltops, canyons, slopes, cliffs, among boulders

Range: Kingcup Hedgehog occurs in most of the northern half of Arizona. Scarlet Hedgehog is present in southeastern Arizona, but also overlaps spottily with Kingcup Hedgehog through parts of central and northern Arizona.

Kingcup Hedgehog
similar radial and single
central spines in Kingcup
and Scarlet

Kingcup Hedgehog
longest spine in Kingcup
and Scarlet does not
have a dark tip

Pink-flowered Hedgehog
(pg. 91)
shorter, dark-tipped
central spines

Compare: Smaller, non-blooming clusters of these two claretcup hedgehogs resemble Pink-flowered Hedgehog (pg. 91), but Pink-flowered does not grow in mounds of hundreds of stems. Pink-flowered has up to four central spines that are dark-tipped and shorter than the longest spines of claretcups. Claretcups are easy to identify in bloom because no other Arizona hedgehogs have such vivid deep red or red-orange flowers.

Notes: Both these hedgehogs are known under a single name, Claretcup Hedgehog, and are the most widespread of the hedgehogs, growing at most elevations and in most life zones in the state except the lowest deserts. Botanists disagree about how to classify claretcup hedgehogs as they are look-alike species, differing in number of chromosomes, with variable characters that can overlap, and distinguishable in the field only by experts. Therefore, we included two widely recognized, main species found in Arizona in this one account. Another species, Arizona Hedgehog, *E. arizonicus*, is very limited in range to southeastern Arizona and in the mountains near Globe.

Unlike other hedgehogs, which are visited mainly by bees, these cacti are pollinated by hummingbirds. Attracted by flower color and copious nectar, hummingbirds fit their whole head into the flowers rather than just their bill.

spines

flower

fruit

Pink-flowered Hedgehog
Echinocereus fasciculatus

Size: H 4–18" (10–45 cm)

Shape: open clumps, up to 24" (61 cm) wide, of 5–30 cylindrical stems

Stem: multiple upright, stout, green stems, each 2–3" (5–7.5 cm) wide, with 10–15 vertical ribs with spines that partially obscure the stem color

Spines: white or gray (often brown or yellow) with dark brown tips, length varies greatly from ³⁄₁₀–3" (.7–7.5 cm) long

Spine Clusters: each cluster has 1–4 central spines pointing outward and upward (1 dark brown central spine is much longer) and 7–15 radial spines pressed against the stem; all spines are straight

Flower: 1 to several rose pink-to-magenta blooms on the sides of stems near the top; each bowl-shaped flower, 2½–4" (6–10 cm) wide, has brown midstripes on outer petals and a center of straw-colored and green flower parts

Blooming: March–April; over a period of several weeks

Fruit: round, spiny, reddish orange pod, ¾–1¼" (2–3 cm) long, with white edible pulp containing many small black seeds

Zone/Habitat: desert scrub, grasslands and interior chaparral from 2,000–6,000' (610–1,830 m); flats, hillsides, bajadas, roadsides, steep canyons, valleys

Range: southeastern corner of Arizona, from the New Mexico border northwest through Safford almost to Winkelman and southwest through Tucson to Sasabe

Bonker Hedgehog *(pg. 75)*
darker magenta flowers

Fendler Hedgehog *(pg. 71)*
fewer and shorter
central spines

Engelmann Hedgehog
(pg. 95)
central spines point
upward

Compare: Resembles Bonker Hedgehog (pg. 75), which is usually shorter, has shorter central spines, and darker magenta-to-purple flowers. Similar to Fendler Hedgehog (pg. 71), but Fendler has fewer and shorter central spines. Engelmann Hedgehog (pg. 95) has more central spines (up to six) that point upward and are can be curved or twisted, unlike the 1–4 straight central spines of Pink-flowered.

Notes: Found only in Arizona, the southwestern corner of New Mexico, and in Sonora, Mexico. Easily seen along Highway 79 between Tucson and Florence, Arizona. The stout stems of this cactus give it another common name, Robust Hedgehog. Spines vary greatly in length from short to long and partially hide the green stems, making the plant appear grayish green and shaggy. Forms clumps of several to more than a couple dozen stems.

Its large, showy blossoms vary from bright pink to magenta like the blooms of several other hedgehog species, so flower color alone is not reliable in identifying this plant. Sometimes judged by botanists to be the same species as Engelmann Hedgehog, *E. engelmannii*, (pg. 95). The longest dark brown central spine in the spine clusters located near the top of the stem is the best way to identify this common hedgehog.

In spring, the stunning flowers of Pink-flowered make the cactus conspicuous in the desert near Tucson. The resulting fruit is eaten by pack rats, ground squirrels, birds, and people.

spines

flower

fruit

Engelmann Hedgehog
Echinocereus engelmannii

Size: H 5½–18" (14–45 cm)

Shape: open or dense clusters, up to 3½' (1.1 m) wide, of 3–60 cylindrical or conical stems

Stem: multiple upright green stems; each stem, 1–3½" (2.5–9 cm) wide, with 10–13 vertical or somewhat wavy ribs with many long spines that obscure the stem color and give the plant a shaggy, almost furry, appearance

Spines: each spine can be a solid color (dull yellow, reddish brown, or white to gray or black), bicolored, or multicolored, ⅓–3" (.8–7.5 cm) long

Spine Clusters: each cluster has 4–6 curved or twisted central spines (lowest and longest is white and points outward and downward) and 6–14 radial spines

Flower: 1 to several funnel-shaped, rosy pink flowers on the sides of stems; each bloom, 2½–3½" (6–9 cm) wide, has petals with darker pink bases around pale yellow and green flower parts

Blooming: March–April; flowers last about 5 days, closing at night and reopening in the morning

Fruit: spiny oval green pod, turning bright red or orange-red when ripe, 1–1¾" (2.5–4.5 cm) long, with sweet, edible, pinkish white pulp containing many small black seeds; when ripe, spines are easy to brush off and pulp tastes like strawberry

Zone/Habitat: desert scrub, pinyon pine/juniper woodlands and interior chaparral from 650–6,000' (200–1,830 m); flats, valleys, ridges, slopes, along washes

Range: western third of Arizona, extending from the Mexico border north to Utah including the area just northwest of Tucson to Phoenix, Prescott and Kingman, to along the North Rim of the Grand Canyon and to Tuba City

Engelmann Hedgehog
longest central spine
is white

Pink-flowered Hedgehog
(pg. 91)
longest central spine is
partly brown

Nichol Hedgehog *(pg. 83)*
all spines are yellow

Compare: Most closely resembles the Pink-flowered Hedgehog (pg. 91), which has 1–4 straight central spines, the longest of which is partly dark brown, unlike Engelmann's longest and lowest, dagger-like central spine, which is white, flattened and somewhat twisted. Engelmann appears shaggier than the Pink-flowered. All spines of the very similar Nichol Hedgehog (pg. 83) are golden yellow.

Notes: The genus *Echinocereus* comes from the Greek *echinos* for "hedgehog" or "spine" and *cereus* for "waxy," referring to the tough green skin of the stems. Botanists continue to argue about how to classify members of this confusing genus and how many species it includes. Currently, it is thought that there are more than a dozen hedgehog species in Arizona. Although variable in flower and spine color, Engelmann is always a very spiny, shaggy hedgehog with spines of multiple colors, large showy flowers, and bright red fruit.

Flowers are open only during the day, so bees do most of the pollinating. When the fruit ripens, the spiny pods turn red and spines become easy to brush off. Fruit is abundant and harvested by southwestern Indigenous tribes in May or June. Also called Strawberry Hedgehog because the fruit tastes something like strawberries. Tiny seeds embedded in the pulp are rich in fat. Fruit is also eaten by birds and rodents.

spines

flower

immature fruit

Many-headed Barrel
Echinocactus polycephalus

Size: H 6–16" (15–40 cm)

Shape: densely packed mounds, up to 3' (.9 m) wide, of 2–50 rounded short stems

Stem: multiple grayish green or yellowish green stems, each 6–12" (15–30 cm) wide, with 11–25 very narrow ribs lined with spines that obscure the stem color and give the plant a shaggy appearance

Spines: red to pale yellow with light tips and covered with an ashy gray felt, 1⅜–5½" (3.5–14 cm) long

Spine Clusters: densely overlapping clusters; each cluster has 4 curved or twisted central spines with horizontal ridges (longest central spine points outward or curves inward) and 6–14 shorter radial spines

Flower: cup-shaped yellow flowers at the top of stem; each bloom, 2¼" (5.5 cm) wide, has layers of petals surrounding bright yellow flower parts; bloom is held partially closed by the spines

Blooming: May–June; perhaps at other times

Fruit: oval green pod, ⅝–1½" (1.5–4 cm) long, with crescent-shaped scales and covered with long, cottony, hair-like white spines; drying to tan when mature and releasing small black seeds through a pore in the base

Zone/Habitat: desert scrub and edges of pinyon pine/juniper woodlands up to 6,500' (1,980 m); rocky slopes, bajadas, ledges of limestone or volcanic rock, canyons, flats among creosote bushes

Range: northwestern quarter of Arizona, from the Utah border east of Page south to the North Rim of the Grand Canyon; also a small area in southwestern Arizona near Yuma

Many-headed Barrel
long, slightly curved
spines and many stems

**Smallflower Fishhook
Cactus** *(pg. 43)*
some central spines
are hooked

**Johnson Pineapple
Cactus** *(pg. 63)*
shorter spines and
a single stem

Compare: Although the single stems of Many-headed Barrel are similar to other barrel cacti, no other barrel cactus forms many-stemmed clumps. Unlike the curved spines of Manyheaded Barrel, some of the central spines of Smallflower Fishhook (pg. 43) are hooked. Johnson Pineapple Cactus (pg. 63) is similar, but has shorter spines and one stem.

Notes: Looks like a cross between a hedgehog and barrel cactus. While any barrel cactus with an injury to the top of its stem may grow 1–2 branches, Many-headed is the only barrel that branches into many stems under normal conditions.

Spines are coated with a gray felt that makes them appear pink or gray unless wet, when they glow bright pink to red. Also called Cottontop Cactus for the woolly white spines on its fruit. Desert birds use the white cotton to build their nests. Pack rats and birds eat the fruit and seeds.

Very slow growing. Twenty-year-old plants raised from seed at the Arizona-Sonoran Desert Museum have just begun to grow more than one stem. Found in Arizona, California, Nevada, and possibly Utah, with range remaining the same for 30,000 years despite the climate change from ice age to hot desert. Grows in the hottest, driest parts of the Mojave, Sonoran and Navajoan Deserts. Can be seen in Grand Canyon National Park.

spines

flower

fruit

Emory Barrel
Ferocactus emoryi

Size: H 12–36" (30–91 cm), some up to 9' (2.7 m); W 12–24" (30–61 cm)

Shape: round or cylindrical cactus with a flat top; taller plants lean southwest

Stem: single stem with 30–32 wide ribs lined with spines; ribs have a shallow notch above each spine cluster

Spines: red, reddish gray, or yellowish gray with yellow tips, 2¼–3¾" (5.5–9.5 cm) long

Spine Clusters: 6–10 stout rigid spines per cluster; each cluster has 1 curving central spine surrounded by radial spines

Flower: cup-shaped, bright red flowers forming a wreath atop the stem; each blossom, 2½–3" (6–7.5 cm) wide, has layers of petals around a center of red flower parts

Blooming: July–September

Fruit: fleshy oval green pod, 1–2" (2.5–5 cm) long, spineless, with crescent-shaped scales on the skin and a brown tuft of leftover dry flower parts on top, turning bright yellow when ripe and releasing small pitted black seeds through a pore at the base

immature cactus

gray notch above each spine cluster

immature fruit

Zone/Habitat: desert scrub from 1,100–4,000' (335–1,220 m); flats, bajadas, rocky hillsides, mesas, arroyos, volcanic gravelly soils

Range: southwestern Arizona, centered around Lukeville east and west along the Mexico border, but also extending north to Mobile through Ajo

Emory Barrel
all spines are stout
and rigid

Fishhook Barrel *(pg. 107)*
bristle-like radial spines

Fishhook Barrel *(pg. 107)*
orange flowers

Compare: Resembles Fishhook Barrel (pg. 107), but lacks its bristle-like white radial spines. All spines of Emory Barrel are stout and rigid with conspicuous horizontal ridges. Fishhook blossoms can be orange to red or yellow, unlike the brilliant red flowers of the Emory that grows in Arizona. Fishhook Barrel is found throughout the range of Emory Barrel.

Notes: There are six species of barrel cacti in the United States, with three in Arizona. All barrel cacti grow cylindrical in shape as they age and resemble the Leaning Tower of Pisa. Faster growth on the shadier side of tall stems causes them to tilt southwest.

An immature Emory Barrel has a rounded, purplish green stem protected by a cage of stout, inward-curving, bright red spines. It has a hooked central spine and lacks well-defined ribs. As it ages, the spines turn gray, the central spine becomes curved and the plant elongates.

Mature cacti flower after the monsoons begin in July, blooming through September. Oval green fruit elongates to cylindrical, turns bright yellow, and remains on the cactus year-round, unless eaten by Mule Deer or desert rodents.

Commonly seen in Organ Pipe Cactus National Monument and in the Tohono O'odham Indian Reservation. Found growing only in Arizona and the western part of the Mexican state of Sonora. In Mexico, the species can have yellow or orange flowers.

105

spines

flower

fruit

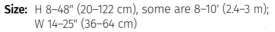

Fishhook Barrel
Ferocactus wislizeni

Size: H 8–48" (20–122 cm), some are 8–10' (2.4–3 m);
W 14–25" (36–64 cm)

Shape: stout round or cylindrical cactus with a flat top;
taller plants lean southwest

Stem: single stem with 20–30 wide vertical ribs lined
with spines that do not obscure the green
stem; ribs have a shallow notch above each
spine cluster

Spines: dull red, gray, tan, or white, 1½–5" (4–13 cm) long

Spine Clusters: each cluster has 2–4 stout central spines (1 is
hooked) with horizontal ridges and 6–16 flexible,
bristle-like radial spines with dark tips

Flower: orange, yellow, or red flowers forming a wreath
atop the stem; each cup-shaped blossom,
1½–3½" (4–9 cm) wide, has layers of petals with
darker midstripes and a center of yellow and
orange flower parts

Blooming: July–October, after summer rains begin; peaks
in August and September; flowering occurs later
than most other cacti

Fruit: fleshy oval green pod, 1⅜–2½" (3.5–6 cm) long,
spineless with scales on the skin and a brown
tuft of leftover dry flower parts on top, turns
bright yellow when ripe and releases small black
seeds through a pore in the base

leaning southwest

Zone/Habitat: desert scrub, grasslands, and lower elevation oak woodlands up to 5,500' (1,675 m); flats, bajadas, rocky hillsides, canyons, limestone or volcanic soils

Range: large portion of southern Arizona, extending east to the New Mexico border, south to the border with Mexico, and west to Hyder and including Safford, Globe, and the area just south of Phoenix; also a small area around Camp Verde in central Arizona

Fishhook Barrel
barrel-shaped stem

Saguaro *(pg. 219)*
club-shaped stem

Saguaro *(pg. 219)*
straight spines

Compare: A tall Fishhook Barrel is sometimes confused with a young Saguaro (pg. 219), but Fishhook has a barrel shape and hooked central spines, unlike the club-shaped immature Saguaro, which has spines that are all straight.

Notes: Barrel cacti are named for their shape and possibly for the mistaken belief that they are hollow and contain water. During the rainy season, the vertical ribs widen and become shallower, allowing the cactus to expand as the plant absorbs water. Storing water enables it to survive many months without rain. If a desperately thirsty desert hiker manages the difficult task of cutting one open, the thick liquid pulp can be consumed, but it has a bad taste.

Fishhook Barrel is a stout, round or barrel-shaped green cactus with reddish gray spines that glow bright red when they get wet. Named for the large, hooked central spine historically used to catch fish. Pulp in the stem was once combined with sugar to make candy. Native wild bees pollinate the flowers. The leathery fruit does not contain pulp and usually is not eaten by people. Fruit stays on the plant even while the first blossoms are opening the next year.

Abundant in southern Arizona, southwestern New Mexico, western Texas, and northern Mexico. Young Fishhooks have stouter spines than mature plants. They start out round and do not lengthen until they are a foot wide. Sometimes older plants over 8 feet (2.4 m) tall tilt southwest so much that the whole cactus uproots and falls over.

spines

flower

fruit

Compass Barrel
Ferocactus acanthodes

Size: H 18–60" (45–152 cm), some are up to 8' (2.4 m); W 10–16" (25–40 cm)

Shape: cylindrical cactus; taller plants lean southwest

Stem: single upright green stem with 21–31 wide vertical ribs; spine-lined ribs have a shallow notch above each spine cluster; spines partially obscure the stem color

Spines: white, yellow, pink, dull red, or brown, 1⅜–5½" (3.5–14 cm) long

Spine Clusters: dense overlapping clusters; each cluster has 4 stout rigid central spines (longest is twisted and points outward and downward) and 8–28 weaker or bristle-like radial spines

Flower: cup-shaped, greenish yellow blooms form a wreath atop the stem; each flower, 1¼–2½" (3–6 cm) wide, has petals with darker midstripes around a center of yellow and red flower parts

Blooming: May–June

Fruit: fleshy cylindrical green pod, turning bright yellow when ripe, 1½" (4 cm) long, crescent-shaped scales on the skin and a brown tuft of leftover dry flower parts on top; spineless, but dense curved central spines on top of the stem protect the pod

immature plant

Zone/Habitat: desert scrub up to 4,900' (1,490 m); rocky slopes of limestone or volcanic rock, ridges, flats, canyons

Range: southwestern Arizona, from Lukeville on the Mexico border north almost to Seligman, east through Winkelman and Tonto Basin, and west to the California border; also the far western edge of the northern half of the state

Compass Barrel
mesh of long tangled
spines obscures the
green stem

Emory Barrel *(pg. 103)*
lacks bristle-like
white spines

Fishhook Barrel *(pg. 107)*
fewer spines and visible
green stem

Compare: Much like Fishhook Barrel (pg. 107), but Compass Barrel often has longer and more numerous central spines that interlock with nearby clusters in a messy tangle, obscuring the green stem. Emory Barrel (pg. 103) lacks bristle-like white spines, a characteristic that Compass shares with Fishhook.

Notes: "Compass" refers to the tendency for older plants to tilt toward the southwest, a trait shared by all species of tall cylindrical barrel cacti in Arizona. Grows in large colonies. Found in Arizona, southern California, southern Nevada, and southwestern Utah in the United States, and Sonora and Baja California in Mexico.

Like all cacti, pores in the green skin of Compass Barrel open only at night, releasing oxygen and letting in carbon dioxide, which it stores as an organic acid. Temperatures are lower and humidity is higher at night, so the plant loses less water. During the day the pores are closed, sealing the plant against water loss, and photosynthesis of nutrients is conducted using the energy from the sun. In severe drought, pores are closed night and day, so photosynthesis and the normal slow growth of the cactus slows even further. The mesh of red and yellow spines and vertical ribs provide shade for the skin, which also decreases water evaporation from the pores. This design permits Compass Barrel to live in an even drier habitat than other barrel cacti. After a rare rainfall, the wet spines glow bright red.

spines

flower

immature fruit

Brittle Prickly Pear
Opuntia fragilis

PRICKLY PEAR

Size: H 1–4" (2.5–10 cm)

Shape: low-growing dense mats, 12–20" (30–50 cm) wide, of globe-shaped, cylindrical, or flat segmented stems

Stem: up to hundreds of stem segments (pads), each ½–2¼" (1–5.5 cm) long and ½–1" (1–2.5 cm) wide and often nearly as thick as wide; pads are knobby and easily detached

Spines: yellow, brown or gray with brown tips, ⅓–9⁄10" (.8–2.4 cm) long

Spine Clusters: diagonal rows of 3–5 clusters across the pad; 3–8 spines per cluster with 1–3 downward-curving spines and inconspicuous crescents of short hair-like brown spines (glochids); clusters are surrounded by woolly white circles

Flower: 1–2 pale greenish yellow flowers atop the upper edges of pads; each bloom, 1–2" (2.5–5 cm) wide, has overlapping, spoon-shaped petals around pale yellow and red flower parts

Blooming: April–June; over a period of several weeks, but blooms only rarely

Fruit: somewhat spiny, fleshy, reddish green pod, drying to tan when ripe, ½–¾" (1–2 cm) long, containing tan seeds

woolly white circles

Zone/Habitat: desert scrub, grasslands, pinyon pine/juniper woodlands, and montane up to 9,000 feet (2,745 m); among sagebrush, barren areas, rocky outcrops, hillsides, flats, sandy or clay soils

Range: northeastern portion of Arizona, ranging from the Utah and New Mexico borders to southwest of Grand Canyon Village on the South Rim of the Grand Canyon, almost to Flagstaff

Brittle Prickly Pear
potato-shaped or thick
pads, not flat like other
prickly pear pads

Hedgehog Prickly Pear
(pg. 131)
thinner pads and
upright clumps

Potts Prickly Pear *(pg. 127)*
immature plants and
other young prickly
pears look like young
Brittle

Compare: Looks somewhat like clumps of Hedgehog Prickly Pear (pg. 131). Brittle has thick pads, unlike other prickly pears in Arizona, but can superficially resemble other species of young prickly pears such as Potts (pg. 127).

Notes: A low-growing prickly pear that blooms infrequently. Flowers are found on it most often when it grows in association with lichens. A lichen cover keeps moisture in the soil, helping flowers to bloom. To propagate, it relies more on the growth of fallen pads rather than on its blossoms and the seeds they produce.

Sometimes called Potato Cactus for the potato-like shape of the pads. The species name *fragilis* refers to these pads, which detach easily. The pads cling to the fur of passing animals and root wherever they drop to the ground, forming new plants. When bison ranged over much of North America, they probably spread this cactus by carrying the pads or fruit on their woolly coats.

Found in the western half of this country in more than 20 states. Ranges farther north than any other cactus species, extending into Canada as far as northern Alberta and British Columbia, where winter temperatures dip to -50 °F (-46 °C). The low mats and thick pads allow this unusual cactus to survive in extreme cold. Low mats are quickly covered and insulated by snow, while the thick pads reduce the ratio of surface area to volume, thus reducing heat loss.

spines

flower

fruit

Plains Prickly Pear
Opuntia polyacantha

Size: H 3–6" (7.5–15 cm)

Shape: low-growing, spreading mats, 12–36" (30–91 cm) wide, of broadly paddle-shaped, flat and segmented stems

Stem: multiple yellowish green stem segments (pads); each pad, 2½–5" (6–13 cm) long and 1½–4" (4–10 cm) wide, is very spiny and firmly attached

Spines: white to gray to reddish brown, ½–1½" (1–4 cm) long

Spine Clusters: diagonal rows of 6–14 clusters across entire pad or only the upper half; 7–18 spines per cluster, pointing outward or downward; spines vary from short and rigid on upper pads to long, curling and thread-like near the base of older pads; inconspicuous crescent of hair-like yellow spines (glochids) above each cluster

Flower: 1 to several yellow blossoms (sometimes pink to red) atop upper edges of pads; each cup-shaped flower, 2–3" (5–7.5 cm) wide, with spoon-shaped petals around a center of yellow flower parts

Blooming: June

Fruit: egg-shaped spiny pod, drying to tan when ripe, ¾–1½" (2–4 cm) long, containing pale tan or white seeds

Zone/Habitat: grasslands and pinyon pine/juniper woodlands between 6,000–7,000' (1,830–2,135 m); among grasses or low trees, on flats, slopes, sandy or gravelly soils

Range: part of northwestern Arizona and the northeastern quarter of the state, from west of Colorado City southeast almost to Eagar and the New Mexico border, and north to the Four Corners, where Arizona, Utah, Colorado, and New Mexico meet

Plains Prickly Pear
shorter, stouter spines

Hedgehog Prickly Pear
(pg. 131)
longer, finer spines

Brown-spine Prickly Pear
(pg. 139)
longer, wider pads and
fewer spines

Compare: Similar to Hedgehog Prickly Pear (pg. 131) in form, but Hedgehog pads are covered with even denser and longer spines than the pads of Plains. Brown-spine Prickly Pear (pg. 139) overlaps in range, but has fewer spines and larger pads.

Notes: Cold tolerant, the hardy Plains Prickly Pear grows throughout western North America from British Columbia and Saskatchewan in Canada, south to Arizona and Texas. In winter, the pads become very wrinkled as cells in the skin lose water, concentrating the salts and other chemicals that are in the sap. This concentrated sap acts like antifreeze in a vehicle radiator, lowering the temperature at which the cells would freeze and suffer damage.

Species name *polyacantha* means "many thorns" in Latin. During drought when grass availability is limited, ranchers will sometimes burn off the cactus spines so their livestock can feed on the pads. Pads sprout roots on the lower edges wherever they touch the ground, giving this spreading cactus its ability to propagate in low dense mats of vegetation that cover large areas.

glochids

flower

fruit

Beavertail Prickly Pear
Opuntia basilaris

Size: H 3–16" (7.5–40 cm)

Shape: low-growing, spreading, trunkless clumps, 3–6' (.9–1.8 m) wide, of flat segmented stems

Stem: multiple bluish green-to-purple stem segments (pads); each pad, 2–9" (5–23 cm) long and 2–5" (5–13 cm) wide, is thick, shaped like a beaver tail, and covered with tiny soft hairs; pads become wrinkled in drought and can make the cactus look dead

Spines: usually spineless, but sometimes a few yellow spines, ⅕–1" (.5–2.5 cm) long

Spine Clusters: diagonal rows of 10–16 circular areas (areoles) across each pad with hair-like yellow or reddish brown spines (glochids) in small round tufts in each areole

Flower: cup-shaped, dark pink flowers on upper edges of pads; each blossom, 3" (7.5 cm) wide, has many overlapping petals around a magenta and pale yellow center

Blooming: February–May; over a period of several weeks

Fruit: spineless, egg-shaped, purplish green pod, 1–1½" (2.5–4 cm) long, covered with tiny velvety hairs, dries to tan when ripe and contains large yellowish tan seeds

immature fruit

Zone/Habitat: desert scrub, oak/pinyon pine/juniper woodlands below 6,000' (1,830 m); open areas, among creosote bushes, rocky hillsides, rock crevices, along washes, valleys, canyons, sandy to gravelly soils

Range: western edge of Arizona, from the Mexico border north through Cibola to the Utah border and as far east as Chino Valley; also a small area of north central Arizona, from the North Rim of the Grand Canyon through Page to the Utah border

Beavertail Prickly Pear
low-growing, spreading clumps

Santa Rita Prickly Pear
(pg. 147)
taller plant with fewer glochid tufts in each row

Santa Rita Prickly Pear
(pg. 147)
yellow flower

Compare: Much like the nearly spineless Santa Rita Prickly Pear (pg. 147) in pad color, but the yellow-flowered Santa Rita has fewer glochid tufts in each row across its pads and is taller and more upright, often with a central trunk.

Notes: A sprawling succulent that seldom grows higher than the length of two pads. The bluish green spineless pads, velvety hairs, and prickly glochids make it easily recognizable. Species name *basilaris*, or "stretching from the base," refers to the paddle-shaped pads in a beaver tail design. In Arizona, the most common variety has rounded or egg-shaped pads.

A favorite landscaping plant in Phoenix and Tucson. Pads turn purple when stressed, making it even more attractive. Grows in the hottest, driest habitat of any prickly pear species in Arizona and is easy to cultivate. To propagate, cut a pad, place in shade for a couple days allowing it to dry and seal, then plant it (cut end down) in a mixture of sand and soil.

Handle the pads carefully! Glochids detach easily and a slight brush against them embeds many nearly invisible barbed spines into skin, where they are hard to see and remove. Embedded glochids impart a burning, prickly sensation. Best removed from skin by placing sticky tape on the affected site and pulling up.

spines

flower

Potts Prickly Pear
Opuntia pottsii

Size: H 8–16" (20–40 cm)

Shape: small shrub, less than 24" (61 cm) wide, of upright or reclining, flat segmented stems

Stem: multiple heart- to diamond-shaped stem segments (pads); each dull dark green or bluish green pad, usually 2½" (6 cm) long, but some up to 8" (20 cm) long, with spines only on the upper half of pad

Spines: all grayish white, sometimes reddish brown, 2–2½" (5–6 cm) long; sometimes spineless

Spine Clusters: diagonal rows of 4–6 clusters only on the upper half of pads; up to 6 slender spines per cluster with hair-like, yellow-to-brownish red spines (glochids) in sparse or dense short tufts

Flower: 8–11 reddish yellow flowers atop the upper edges of pads; each cup-shaped blossom, 2½" (6 cm) wide, has inner yellow petals tinged red or all-red petals around pale yellow flower parts; flower buds are peach-colored

Blooming: May–June; over a period of several weeks

Fruit: oval fleshy pod, green to yellow to dull red, 1–1½" (2.5–4 cm) long, with few spines or spineless, containing tan seeds

Zone/Habitat: desert scrub, grasslands, and oak woodlands from 2,600–6,000' (795–1,830 m); flats, slopes, sandy to loamy soils

Range: most of the northern half of Arizona; also the southeastern corner of the state, extending almost to San Manuel

Potts Prickly Pear
white spines only on
upper half of smaller
pads

Brown-spine Prickly Pear
(pg. 139)
larger plant and
larger pads

Black-spine Prickly Pear
(pg. 135)
much longer spines

Compare: Resembles Brown-spine Prickly Pear (pg. 139), but Potts is overall smaller and has lots of all-white spines on its smaller pads. Also similar to Black-spine Prickly Pear (pg. 135), but Black-spine is somewhat larger and has much longer spines.

Notes: Stems of all prickly pears grow in jointed segments (pads) and have spine clusters with many minute barbed bristles (glochids) as well as spines. Glochids are present only on prickly pear and cholla cacti. Each new pad grows during the summer monsoons from a spine cluster on an old pad, starting as a bud displaying tiny ephemeral leaves. Prickly pear cacti are sometimes called flat-stemmed opuntias. This distinguishes them from the chollas, which are known as round-stemmed opuntias.

Potts is a small prickly pear with upright pads, tuberous roots containing milky white juice, and spines that often twist spirally. Once thought to be a variety of Twist-spine Prickly Pear (not shown), which is widespread, but not believed to be in Arizona. Potts is the only prickly pear in Arizona that sometimes has all-red flowers.

Easily seen occupying vacant lots in Wilcox and along the San Pedro River, a rare and ecologically important riparian habitat in southeastern Arizona. Potts is also commonly seen in far western Texas, southern New Mexico, and Chihuahua, Mexico, but isolated plants have been found as far east as Missouri and Wisconsin.

129

spines

flower

immature fruit

Hedgehog Prickly Pear
Opuntia erinacea

Size: H 8–24" (20–61 cm)

Shape: low-growing clumps, 24–36" (61–91 cm) wide, of thick and paddle-shaped or egg-shaped segmented stems

Stem: multiple upright, dull green to dull red stem segments (pads); each pad, 2–5" (5–13 cm) long and 1–3" (2.5–7.5 cm) wide, covered with numerous spines of varying length

Spines: white to pale yellow with yellowish brown bases, 1–7" (2.5–18 cm) long

Spine Clusters: 4–24 flexible spines per cluster; 3 or more lowest spines shorter and turning strongly downward; thread-like spines on older pads are much longer and more numerous; tiny crescent of hair-like yellow spines (glochids) above each cluster

Flower: light yellow flowers (outer petal tips tinged bronze or red) on the upper edges of pads; each cup-shaped blossom, 2" (5 cm) wide, has spoon-shaped petals and yellow and green flower parts

Blooming: May–June; over a period of several weeks

Fruit: barrel-shaped green pod tinged with red, 1–1½" (2.5–4 cm) long, drying to tan when mature and becoming bur-like, covered with short rigid spines and containing small dark brown or yellow seeds

Zone/Habitat: desert scrub and pinyon pine/juniper woodlands between 1,500–7,000' (460–2,135 m); among creosote bushes, sagebrush or pine scrub, gravelly or rocky slopes

Range: northwestern corner of Arizona, from south of Needles on the California border to east of Kaibab; especially on the North and South Rims of the Grand Canyon

Hedgehog Prickly Pear
spinier, with longer
flexible spines

Plains Prickly Pear *(pg. 119)*
flower petals are all pink
or all yellow

Brown-spine Prickly Pear
(pg. 139)
fewer spines

Compare: Much like the low-growing, spreading Plains Prickly Pear (pg. 119) in form, but Plains has fewer, shorter spines and all-pink or all-yellow flower petals. Brown-spine Prickly Pear (pg. 139) also has fewer spines than Hedgehog.

Notes: Prickly pears are the most common and widespread cacti. While they are always easy to recognize by their round flat pads, they can be difficult to further identify due to large variations within many species and frequent hybridization between species. When one species hybridizes with others and produces plants with intermediate characteristics, the resulting crosses are even harder to identify.

Sometimes considered by botanists to be a subspecies of Plains Prickly Pear (pg. 119), the species name *erinacea* means "hedgehog" and refers to a European animal that has spines. Hedgehog Prickly Pear forms in small low clumps. It has very spiny green pads that turn reddish brown during winter. Cold tolerant, it is the most common prickly pear in the pinyon pine/juniper woodlands of northwestern Arizona.

Hedgehog is sometimes called Grizzlybear Prickly Pear for the grizzled appearance of its shaggy white spines. This interesting-looking cactus is often cultivated.

133

spines

flower

fruit

Black-spine Prickly Pear
Opuntia macrocentra

Size: H 12–36" (30–91 cm)

Shape: low-growing shrub, 2–4' (61–122 cm) wide, of upright or reclining, broad paddle-shaped or circular segmented stems

Stem: multiple bluish green stem segments (pads) with a tinge of purple on edges and around spine clusters; each flattened pad, 3–8" (7.5–20 cm) long and 2½–7" (6–18 cm) wide; entire pad turns nearly red in cold or drought

Spines: spineless or 3–7" (7.5–18 cm) long, reddish brown to black with white tips; long spines turn gray with age

Spine Clusters: diagonal rows of 6–8 clusters across each pad or only on the upper edges; up to 3 spines per cluster; spines are very long, thin and flexible; some clusters have hair-like, reddish yellow spines (glochids) in short, crescent-shaped, pointed tufts

Flower: 1–8 yellow-and-red flowers atop the upper edges of pads; each cup-shaped bloom, 2–3" (5–7.5 cm) wide, with lower inner half of petals tinged dark red around pale yellow flower parts

Blooming: April–June; over a period of several weeks

Fruit: barrel-shaped, red or purple pod, 1–1½" (2.5–4 cm) long, smooth, spineless, and fleshy, with tan seeds

Zone/Habitat: desert scrub and grasslands from 2,000–6,000' (610–1,830 m); flats, hills, valleys, sandy to rocky soils

Range: southeastern corner of Arizona, from the Mexico and New Mexico borders northwest to just north of Eloy

Black-spine Prickly Pear
longer, darker spines

Brown-spine Prickly Pear
(pg. 139)
shorter, lighter spines

Santa Rita Prickly Pear
(pg. 147)
taller plant with shorter
spines or lacks spines

Compare: Resembles Brown-spine Prickly Pear (pg. 139), but Black-spine has longer, darker spines. Also similar to Santa Rita Prickly Pear (pg. 147) in color, especially when stressed, but Black-spine is a shorter plant with longer spines.

Notes: A short shrub with yellow-and-red flowers and thin flexible spines, usually found only along the upper edges of the pads. Often called Long-spine Prickly Pear for the length of its spines—the longest of any cactus species in Arizona. The species name *macro-centra* refers to the longest central spine in the uppermost spine clusters. Interestingly, while known for its long spines, there is a Black-spine variety that lacks spines.

Pads are bluish green with tinges of purple on the edges during monsoon rains, but when stressed by cold or drought, the entire pad will turn all purple to nearly red. Sometimes named Purple Prickly Pear. The yellow-and-red flowers or red fruit against the green or purple pads combined with the neat appearance of this small cactus make it a favorite of desert landscapers.

Although this species extends south into Mexico, in the United States it is found only in Arizona, New Mexico, and Texas.

spines

flower

fruit

Brown-spine Prickly Pear
Opuntia phaeacantha

PRICKLY PEAR

Size: H 12–36" (30–91 cm)

Shape: low sprawling clumps, 3–8' (.9–2.4 m) wide, of paddle-shaped to circular segmented stems

Stem: multiple light green-to-bluish green stem segments (pads); each pad, 4–10" (10–25 cm) long and 3–8" (7.5–20 cm) wide, is flat and firmly attached; sometimes purple on pad edges and around spine clusters, especially in winter

Spines: reddish brown or brown and white, 1–3" (2.5–7.5 cm) long

Spine Clusters: diagonal rows of 5–7 clusters across the pad; each cluster with up to 9 straight, curved, or twisted spines (longer and denser on upper two-thirds of pad, no spines or a few shorter ones lower on pad); dense hair-like brown spines (glochids) in tufts at top of each cluster

Flower: 1 to several yellow flowers (sometimes pink or salmon), turning orange with age, atop the upper edges of pads; each tulip-shaped bloom, 2–2½" (5–6 cm) wide, has petals with red bases and wavy edges around pale yellow flower parts

Blooming: April–June; over a period of several weeks

Fruit: barrel-shaped red-to-purple pod, 1–2" (2.5–5 cm) long, few spines or spineless, with glochids at the base of pod; fleshy green pulp is edible, containing large tan seeds

cochineal insect webs

Zone/Habitat: desert scrub, grasslands, oak/pinyon pine/juniper woodlands and interior chaparral between 2,000–8,000' (610–2,440 m); open areas, among grasses or creosote bushes, rocky hillsides, rock crevices, along washes, valleys, canyons, sandy to gravelly well-drained soils

Range: eastern two-thirds of Arizona, extending from the Utah border south to the border with Mexico and west through Marana, Wickenberg, and Kingman, but east of Phoenix

Engelmann Prickly Pear
(pg. 151)
shorter white spines

Engelmann Prickly Pear
(pg. 151)
inner base of flower petals is not red

Black-spine Prickly Pear
(pg. 135)
longer spines and fewer glochids

Compare: Much like Engelmann Prickly Pear (pg. 151) with which it often hybridizes, making identification difficult. Engelmann is a taller, more robust cactus than Brown-spine, usually having shorter white spines on its pads, no red at the base of its inner flower petals, red pulp inside the fruit (instead of green), and lacking the purple pad edges that Brown-spine sometimes has. Brown-spine has shorter spines and more glochids than the similar Black-spine Prickly Pear (pg. 135).

Notes: A very widespread, common cactus across the West from California to Texas, Kansas, and Oklahoma and into Mexico. The tulip shape of the flower gives this species another name, Tulip Prickly Pear. Often called Sprawling Prickly Pear for its habit of trailing along the ground, the pads root wherever they touch the soil, forming chains of plants. Newly sprouted during the summer monsoons, the pads are first red, turning green with age.

Prickly pear fruit and pads are high in pectin, which may lower cholesterol in humans, and are also high in slowly absorbed soluble fibers that help keep blood sugar in diabetics stable. A parasitic cochineal insect can infest prickly pears, covering the pads with cottony white webs. Carminic acid, extracted from the insects to make a bright red dye (carmine), is used to color food, drugs, and cosmetics.

141

spines

flower

immature fruit

Spineless Prickly Pear
Opuntia laevis

Size: H 2–6' (.6–1.8 m)

Shape: spreading shrubby cactus, up to 8' (2.4 m) wide, with paddle-shaped segmented stems

Stem: multiple shiny stem segments (pads); each pad, 6–10" (15–25 cm) long and 4½–6" (11–15 cm) wide, is smooth, thin, and flat

Spines: few to no spines, grayish white when present, ½" (1 cm) long

Spine Clusters: diagonal rows of widely spaced tufts of hair-like yellow spines (glochids) across the pad

Flower: 1 to several yellow flowers, turning orange with age, atop the upper edges of pads; each tulip-shaped blossom, 2–3" (5–7.5 cm) wide, has overlapping petals, sometimes with red bases surrounding pale yellow flower parts

Blooming: April–May; over a period of several weeks

Fruit: cylindrical, mostly spineless pod with a narrow base, turning dark purplish red when ripe, 2¾–3¼" (7–8 cm) long, smooth and fleshy, containing large tan seeds

Zone/Habitat: desert scrub, grasslands, and oak woodlands from 2,800–4,000' (855–2,440 m); steep rocky slopes, rock crevices, cliffs, valleys with deeper soils

Range: portion of southeastern Arizona, from just west of Tucson to east of Wilcox, north through Roosevelt, and south to the Mexico border

Spineless Prickly Pear
pads have glochids

Barbary Fig (pg. 159)
smooth pads usually
lack glochids

Barbary Fig (pg. 159)
woody central trunk

Compare: Much like the spineless Barbary Fig (pg. 159), but is not as large and upright and does not have a woody brown central trunk. Spineless usually has glochids on its pads, while Barbary rarely does.

Notes: This was once considered a variety of Brown-spine Prickly Pear (pg. 139), resembling it closely in shape and size; however, the spines of Brown-spine makes it easy to distinguish from Spineless. Also called Smooth Prickly Pear or Tulip Prickly Pear.

A smooth, spreading cactus with only glochids for defense, this plant provides easy pickings for javelinas, deer, and cattle. It's therefore usually seen on inaccessible cliffs, steep rocky slopes, and in rock crevices, all of which are hard for large animals to reach.

Not very common in the wild, limited in range to parts of Arizona, southwestern New Mexico, and northern Sonora, Mexico. Seen in Box Canyon in the Santa Rita Mountains, south of Tucson. Cultivated as fodder for livestock and also for erosion control. The amount of protein in the pads is low, making it an incomplete food for cattle.

The first specimen of this species was collected in May 1881 by C. G. Pringle, a botanist who explored Arizona from 1881–84. Interestingly, this same specimen remains and is stored in the Missouri Botanical Garden Herbarium in St. Louis.

spines

flower

fruit

Santa Rita Prickly Pear
Opuntia santa-rita

Size: H 4–7' (1.2–2.1 m)

Shape: upright and shrubby or tree-like (often has a short trunk), with flat segmented stems

Stem: multiple bluish green-to-purple stem segments (pads); each pad, 4–8" (10–20 cm) wide, is smooth, thin, and round with few spines; pad edges are tinged with purple during monsoons; entire pad turns lavender to purple when stressed by drought or cold

Spines: spineless or pinkish white to reddish brown, often shorter than 1½" (4 cm) long

Spine Clusters: diagonal rows of 6–8 round or crescent-shaped tufts of hair-like, yellow-to-brown spines (glochids) across the pad; 1 cylindrical, needle-tipped spine in a few circular areas (areoles) on the upper edges of the pads

Flower: 1–5 bright lemon yellow flowers, fading to apricot, atop the upper edges of pads; each cup-shaped bloom, 2–3½" (5–9 cm) wide, has overlapping petals with wavy edges surrounding yellow and green flower parts

Blooming: April–early June; over a period of several weeks

Fruit: smooth, spineless, barrel-shaped pod, 1–2" (2.5–5 cm) long, pale reddish purple when ripe, has fleshy green pulp and large tan seeds

Zone/Habitat: desert scrub, grasslands, and oak woodlands from 3,000–5,000' (915–1,525 m); flats, slopes, bajadas, valleys, sandy to rocky soils

Range: small area of central southern Arizona, from south of Tucson to Nogales along both sides of Interstate 10, including the Santa Rita Mountains

Santa Rita Prickly Pear
thinner pad and rusty or
pinkish white spines

Beavertail Prickly Pear
(pg. 123)
thicker pads and yellow
spines or spineless

Black-spine Prickly Pear
(pg. 135)
red base on inner petals

Compare: At first glance, Santa Rita looks much like Beavertail Prickly Pear (pg. 123). Beavertail is a shorter, always sprawling, trunkless bush that has thicker pads with more closely spaced glochid tufts and yellow spines (when they are present), not reddish brown like those of Santa Rita. Santa Rita is also commonly confused with the spineless form of Black-spine Prickly Pear (pg. 135), but Black-spine inner flower petals have red bases.

Notes: A shrubby prickly pear with thin flat pads or tree-like with a short trunk. Named for the Santa Rita Mountains in the northeastern portion of its range. An attractive cactus, it is most easily recognized by its mostly spineless, lavender or purple pads with many prickly glochids. Newly sprouted pads are dark red-purple.

Often cultivated, but does not tolerate cold or drought very well. In addition, its spineless pads are nearly defenseless and usually eaten by rodents and livestock. The glochids can be dangerous, as they are loosely fixed to pads and often fly off when the plant is handled, sometimes getting into the eyes of people or pets.

Found in central southern Arizona and northern Mexico. In Arizona, it sometimes hybridizes with Pancake Prickly Pear (pg. 155), which has numerous yellow spines.

white spines

yellow spines

flower

Engelmann Prickly Pear
Opuntia engelmannii

Size: H 3–10' (.9–3 m)

Shape: shrubby, mostly trunkless cactus of tall spreading clumps, 6–15' (1.8–4.6 m) wide, with large flat segmented stems

Stem: multiple dull yellowish green or bluish green stem segments (pads); each pad, 6–16" (15–40 cm) long and 4–16" (10–40 cm) wide, is oblong, circular or diamond-shaped, with short spines; pads are firmly attached

Spines: chalky white, sometimes yellow, ½–1" (1–2.5 cm) long

Spine Clusters: diagonal rows of 5–8 clusters widely spaced across the pad; 1–6 stout flat spines per cluster, pointing outward or bent abruptly downward; hair-like, yellow-to-reddish brown spines (glochids) in irregular tufts surround each cluster

Flower: lemon yellow flowers, turning apricot with age, covering the upper edges of pads; each showy, cup-shaped bloom, 3" (7.5 cm) wide, has petals with wavy blunt edges around yellow and green flower parts; produces loads of blossoms when winter rains have been heavy

Blooming: April–May; over a period of several weeks

Fruit: barrel-shaped green pod, 1½–3½" (4–9 cm) long, lacks large spines but has glochids; turning dark red when ripe with juicy, edible, dark red pulp, containing tan or gray flat seeds

fruit

new pad

Cow's Tongue

Zone/Habitat: desert scrub, grasslands and oak/pine/juniper woodlands from 1,500–6,000' (460–1,830 m); ridges, slopes, flats, along washes, valleys, canyons, sandy to gravelly soils

Range: southern Arizona and the southeastern part of the state from Lukeville to Clifton; extending northwest in a broad band through Phoenix to Kingman and Seligman in northern Arizona and ranging northeast in a narrower band past Supai

Engelmann Prickly Pear
short white spines and
many glochids

Brown-spine Prickly Pear
(pg. 139)
brown spines

Black-spine Prickly Pear
(pg. 135)
longer spines and
fewer glochids

Compare: Much like Brown-spine Prickly Pear (pg. 139), with which it hybridizes. Engelmann spines are usually short and white, not like the reddish brown or brown and white spines of Brown-spine. Black-spine Prickly Pear (pg. 135) has longer spines and fewer glochids than Engelmann.

Notes: Common in the Southwest and northern Mexico. The most abundant and variable prickly pear in southern Arizona, especially in deserts around Tucson and Phoenix. Recognizable by its large pads, widely spreading tall form and short white spines. Readily sprouts roots and a new plant from each pad that touches the ground, forming impenetrable thickets. Sometimes has a short, central woody stem. Cow's Tongue Prickly Pear, a unique variety cultivated in desert landscaping in Phoenix and Tucson, has tongue-shaped pads as long as 45 inches (114 cm). Another variety with yellow spines occurs only in Arizona and is found in western parts of the Engelmann range.

New lime green pads with tiny conical leaves face east and west for longer exposure to the sun during monsoon season. Young spine-less pads can be cooked as a vegetable. Also called Cactus Apple for its fruit, from which juice and jams are made. Pack rats eat the fruit and build nest mounds in the midst of Engelmann clumps, using the spiny pads to form a protective barrier.

spines

flower

fruit

Pancake Prickly Pear
Opuntia chlorotica

Size: H 6½–8' (2–2.4 m)

Shape: upright shrub or tree-like, Y-shaped cactus with a distinctive spiny, knobby trunk and thick flat segmented stems

Stem: multiple grayish green or bluish green stem segments (pads); each pad, 5–8" (13–20 cm) long, is pancake-shaped or oval and has several to many spines on the outer two-thirds of pads

Spines: spineless or yellow, aging to reddish brown, 1–1¾" (2.5–4.5 cm) long

Spine Clusters: diagonal rows of 7–10 clusters across the outer two-thirds of pads; each cluster has up to 7 unequal-length spines, flattened at their bases and pointing downward, several fine bristle-like spines and a narrow, crescent-shaped tuft of hair-like yellow spines (glochids)

Flower: 1–5 yellow flowers tinged with red, atop the upper edges of pads; each cup-shaped bloom, 1½–2½" (4–6 cm) wide, has overlapping petals with middle veins outlined in red, around pale yellow flower parts

Blooming: April–May; over a period of several weeks

Fruit: barrel-shaped red pod, 1½–2½" (4–6 cm) long, smooth, spineless and fleshy, containing large tan seeds

spines on upper
portions of pad

trunk

Zone/Habitat: desert scrub, grasslands, and oak woodlands from 2,000–6,000' (610–1,830 m); desert flats, slopes, ledges, rock out-crops, canyons, sandy to rocky soils

Range: broad band from southeastern to northwestern Arizona, covering about half of the state

Pancake Prickly Pear
spinier pad

Santa Rita Prickly Pear
(pg. 147)
purple pad and
fewer spines

Santa Rita Prickly Pear
(pg. 147)
overall shape resembles
Pancake

Compare: Resembles Santa Rita Prickly Pear (pg. 147), sharing a tree-like spreading form on a short trunk, but Pancake pads are spinier and bluish green rather than purple.

Notes: Pancake Prickly Pear is named for its rounded flat pads. The species name *chlorotica* means "yellowish green" and refers to its yellow spines and glochids, which often give the plant a fuzzy, golden appearance. It has a thick round trunk that is uniquely spiny and knobby and has pads that become spinier with age.

A hardy prickly pear, it is tolerant of fire, resprouting from its base. Often grows on ledges high on canyon walls in the mountains or among rock outcrops. Sometimes hybridizes with Santa Rita Prickly Pear.

Like all cacti, this plant lacks leaves, photosynthesizing its food through the smooth green skin of its pads. In addition to the defensive spines, the fleshy pads are protected with a layer of calcium oxalate crystals, which is toxic to the kidneys of animals that eat the pads (with the exception of javelinas, pack rats, and desert tortoises). These animals have kidneys that somehow can tolerate the sharp crystals.

Can be seen on the desert flats near Aquila, northwest of Phoenix. Less common in the southern part of the state.

spineless areoles

flower

fruit

Barbary Fig
Opuntia ficus-indica

Size: H 10–20' (3–6.1 m)

Shape: massive tree-like cactus with a spineless trunk, 14–18" (36–45 cm) wide, branches spreading to 10' (3 m) wide, and numerous segmented pads

Stem: multiple smooth, glossy, light green stem segments (pads); each pad, 8–24" (20–61 cm) long, broadly oblong or oval, lacking spines

Spines: usually spineless; if present, white to brown, less than 1/10" (.2 cm) long, occasionally up to 1½" (4 cm) long

Spine Clusters: rarely several clusters on upper edges of pads; each cluster has up to 6 awl-shaped or bristle-like spines; sometimes has 7–11 tiny tufts of hair-like yellow spines (glochids) in diagonal rows across the pad

Flower: yellowish orange or red flowers on the upper edges of pads; each cup-shaped blossom, 2–3½" (5–9 cm) wide, has overlapping petals surrounding yellow and red flower parts

Blooming: April–early June; over a period of several weeks

Fruit: pink-to-purple (often yellow) pod, 2–4" (5–10 cm) long, barrel-shaped, smooth, nearly spineless, fleshy, and juicy, containing large tan seeds

Zone/Habitat: desert scrub between 2,500–3,000' (760–915 m); gardens, yards, vacant lots, highway medians, near old buildings, desert flats

Range: small area in southeastern Arizona, from in and around Tucson to south of Green Valley and west of Three Points

Barbary Fig
spineless trunk

Pancake Prickly Pear
(pg. 155)
spiny trunk

Spineless Prickly Pear
(pg. 143)
pad with glochids

Compare: Somewhat resembles the trunked form of Pancake Prickly Pear (pg. 155), but Pancake always has glochid clusters covering the surface of its pads, and its trunk is spiny. Barbary Fig is taller, with smooth pads and lacks spines on its woody trunk. Spineless Prickly Pear (pg. 143) has glochids.

Notes: An introduced, spineless, tree-like cactus that was most likely domesticated long ago by people in central Mexico. Probably exported in the 1500s to Lisbon, Portugal, from where it spread to warm climates around the world. In Arizona, it has naturalized to the wild around Tucson. Grows rapidly, as much as 6 feet (1.8 m) during a Tucson summer, with widely spreading branches of numerous large pads.

Cultivated for its spineless pads (*nopalitos* in Spanish). Young pads can be boiled, pickled, or eaten as a salad. Studies show that consumption of these young pads reduces blood sugar levels in some diabetics and reduces the symptoms of alcohol hangover. Pads are also used for raising parasitic cochineal insects, which are dried and pulverized to make a natural red or purple dye. *Tunas*, the Spanish name for the large, sweet, juicy fruit, make delicious syrups, jellies, and jams. In Mexico, the pads and fruit are used to feed livestock.

Sometimes known as Mission Fig, since long ago it was planted at Spanish missions in the Southwest. At that time, the stem pulp was mixed with clay to make adobe bricks for missions.

spines

flower

fruit

Devil Cholla
Grusonia kunzei

Size: H 6–20" (15–50 cm)

Shape: large spreading mats, up to 12' (3.7 m) wide, branching near the ground into upright segmented stems

Stem: multiple green stem segments (joints), each 4–6" (10–15 cm) long, club-shaped and curved with large conspicuous knobs (tubercles) and dense spines that nearly hide the stem color; segments are not easily detached

Spines: reddish tan to gray, 1–2" (2.5–5 cm) long

Spine Clusters: dense interlacing clusters; each cluster has 17–27 stout spines of varying length, with the lower 4–6 spines flattened and bent downward; hair-like yellow spines (glochids) in sparse tufts at the top of each cluster

Flower: 1–5 yellow-to-yellowish green flowers clustered at the tips of stems; each cup-shaped bloom, 1–2" (2.5–5 cm) wide, has overlapping petals and a wide, fuzzy, pale yellow center; a deciduous leaf grows just below the flower

Blooming: May–June

Fruit: spiny, fleshy, pear-shaped yellow fruit, 1½–3" (4–7.5 cm) long, with 6–17 yellow-to-brown spines per cluster and large glochids, contains pale seeds; fruit is abundant on this cholla

Zone/Habitat: desert scrub up to 1,500' (460 m); flats, valleys, hills, dunes, among creosote bushes

Range: southwestern part of Arizona, from the Mexico border north to Highway 93 through Quartzsite and Aquila

Devil Cholla
segmented stem

Engelmann Hedgehog
(pg. 95)
undivided stems

Teddy Bear Cholla *(pg. 171)*
tree-like trunk

Compare: The mats of Devil Cholla superficially resemble giant clumps of hedgehog cacti, but Devil stems are segmented and have elongated knobs (tubercles), unlike hedgehog stems, which are undivided with vertical ridges (ribs). Devil Cholla lacks the trunk that characterizes other tree-like chollas such as Teddy Bear Cholla (pg. 171).

Notes: There are eight species of club chollas in the Southwest. Club chollas are easily recognized by the way they branch near the ground and form creeping mats. Very much alike, they differ only in stem size, spine cluster pattern, flower color and number of spines on fruit. Called "club" for the stem segment shape—narrow at the base, thicker on top with noticeably knobby tubercles. Four of these species grow in Arizona, with Devil Cholla the most common and conspicuous.

Devil Cholla grows only in the Sonoran Desert of Arizona (where it is common in the Cabeza Prieta National Wildlife Refuge) and the Mexican states of Sonora and Baja California. Can be seen along Interstate 10 between Phoenix and the Colorado River. It forms a dense ground cover that can carpet large areas and is impossible to walk through. These impenetrable, spiny areas are the reason it has been commonly attributed to the devil. When dead, its hollow, net-like, woody skeleton resembles those of the taller chollas in the *Cylindropuntia* genus.

high growth form

spines

flower

immature fruit

Whipple Cholla
Cylindropuntia whipplei

Size: H 4–7' (1.2–2.1 m) or more commonly, 12–24" (30–61 cm)

Shape: upright and tree-like with a short trunk or grow- ing in low, widely spreading clumps; both forms with many short segmented stems

Stem: multiple green-to-purple stem segments (joints), each 1–6" (2.5–15 cm) long, with prominent oval bumps (tubercles) that are about 3 times longer than they are wide; stems are spinier toward the tips, but spines do not obscure the color of stems

Spines: whitish pink or pale yellow, ¾–2" (2–5 cm) long

Spine Clusters: overlapping clusters; 3–8 spines per cluster (1 to several shorter spines around the long upright central spines); hair-like yellow spines (glochids) in a small tuft next to the spine cluster

Flower: greenish yellow flowers at the tips of stems; each narrowly cup-shaped flower, ¾–1½" (2–4 cm) wide, has overlapping spoon-shaped petals with sharp tips around bright yellowish green flower parts

Blooming: June–July; over a period of several weeks

Fruit: broadly cone-shaped, reddish green pod, turning yellow, ⅔–1" (1.6–2.5 cm) long, spineless, with very knobby, fleshy skin; pod stays on the cactus throughout winter

low growth form covered with ripe fruit

Zone/Habitat: desert scrub, grasslands, oak/pinyon pine/juniper woodlands, and montane between 3,000–8,000' (915–2,440 m); high mesas, among sagebrush, pine clearings, flats, drainages

Range: northern half of Arizona except the far western edge, from Kingman northeast to near Colorado City and east to Heber

Whipple Cholla
less spiny stem

Golden Cholla (pg. 175)
spinier stem

Golden Cholla (pg. 175)
dry spiny fruit

Compare: Most like Golden Cholla (pg. 175), which has much spinier stems and dry spiny fruit, unlike the fleshy spineless fruit of Whipple Cholla.

Notes: This cholla has two growth forms: a low-growing mat of upright stems (the most abundant form) or an upright, slender, tree-like, slow-growing cactus. Cold hardy, growing at higher elevations than most other chollas in Arizona. Also called Plateau Cholla for the high mesas where it grows.

The Hopi, an Indigenous tribe living in the Four Corners area of Arizona, Utah, Colorado, and New Mexico for at least a thousand years, historically ate the fruit of this cactus and used it to season other foods. The fruit and young branches are a favorite food of Pronghorn, fleet-footed antelope that graze in open grasslands.

Especially common south of Winslow and in Canyon de Chelly National Monument, the traditional home of the Navajo, located near Chinle, Arizona.

spines

flower

immature fruit

Teddy Bear Cholla
Cylindropuntia bigelovii

Size: H 1–5' (30–152 cm)

Shape: short cactus with a single trunk topped with thick, cylindrical, segmented stems (rarely branching)

Stem: multiple short stem segments (joints), appearing fuzzy and golden yellow, each 1½–5" (4–13 cm) long, with dense spines that totally obscure the green stem color and the broad oval bumps (tubercles), making older, lower branches look dark; segments detach easily

Spines: pale yellow, turning brown to black with age, ⅝–1" (1.5–2.5 cm) long

Spine Clusters: densely packed, interlacing clusters; each cluster has 10–15 spines of uniform length; hair-like yellow spines (glochids) form a crescent-shaped tuft above each cluster

Flower: 1–2 green-to-greenish yellow flowers at the tips of stems; each cup-shaped flower, 1" (2.5 cm) wide, has overlapping, spoon-shaped petals (sometimes red-tipped) around mostly green flower parts

Blooming: March–June and again in September after the summer rains; over a period of several weeks

Fruit: spiny green pod, ¾–1½" (2–4 cm) long, with very prominent bumps (tubercles); turning yellow, leathery, and spineless when ripe; often infertile; fertile pods contain tiny pale yellow seeds in a jelly-like mass

fruit

Zone/Habitat: desert scrub and grasslands between 500–3,000' (150–915 m); on rocky slopes, along washes, flats, in sandy or gravelly soils

Range: southwestern Arizona, from Bullhead City south to Lukeville and east to Tucson and Winkelman; also a small area in the north-western corner of the state

Teddy Bear Cholla
short stem segments

Jumping Cholla *(pg. 203)*
longer stem segments

Jumping Cholla *(pg. 203)*
immature plant

Compare: Most like Jumping Cholla (pg. 203), which grows taller, has longer stem segments and chains of fruit that remain on the plant for years. Fruit of Teddy Bear Cholla doesn't stay on the plant for long. Prior to fruiting, immature Jumping Cholla cacti look much like Teddy Bear plants.

Notes: A short, compact cholla, with pale yellow spines so dense and uniform that the plant appears cute and fuzzy from a distance, hence the common name "Teddy Bear." When backlit with early morning or late afternoon light, the spines glow as though lit from within.

Stem segments drop off readily, littering the ground around the plant, sprouting roots and growing into new plants. Pack rats gather the spiny stems to roof their mounded nests, using them as a defense against predators.

Native to areas with less than 4 inches (10 cm) of rain, this little cactus nevertheless forms dense stands that can cover large areas of desert. Desert hikers usually avoid these patches due to the difficulty of passing through without getting punctured. Occurs in Arizona, Nevada, California, and south into Mexico.

173

spines

flower

fruit

Golden Cholla
Cylindropuntia echinocarpa

Size: H 3–4' (.9–1.2 m)

Shape: bushy with a squat trunk and short branching stems divided into cylindrical stem segments

Stem: multiple stem segments (joints), appearing pale yellow, each 1¼–6" (3–15 cm) long, drooping or horizontal, with many prominent bumps (tubercles) that are twice as long as they are wide and dense spines that cover the dull green or purple color of the stems; segments are firmly attached

Spines: white to yellow, ¾–2" (2–5 cm) long

Spine Clusters: overlapping clusters; each cluster has 10–17 spines of unequal length, with 1 much longer spine; conspicuous broad crescent of hair-like yellow spines (glochids) above each cluster

Flower: 1 to several greenish yellow (sometimes red) flowers at the tips of stems; each cup-shaped blossom, 2½" (6 cm) wide, has a center of yellow flower parts and sometimes has red splotches on outer yellow petals

Blooming: March–May; over a period of several weeks

Fruit: teardrop-shaped green pod, ½–⅞" (1–2.3 cm) long, with very large protuberances (tubercles) and dense spines with barbs, remaining spiny and drying to tan when mature, containing pale yellow seeds

Zone/Habitat: desert scrub, grasslands, oak/juniper woodlands up to 5,000' (1,525 m); flats, slopes, along washes

Range: western edge of Arizona, extending from the northern border with Utah, south to the boundary with Mexico, and east almost to Aquila

Golden Cholla
varying-length spines

Teddy Bear Cholla *(pg. 171)*
uniform-length spines

Buckhorn Cholla *(pg. 191)*
narrower tubercles

Compare: Short Golden Cholla individuals can resemble Teddy Bear Cholla (pg. 171), which differs by its stem spines of nearly uniform length and fruit that loses its spines when ripe. Can also resemble Buckhorn Cholla (pg. 191), which is found in its range in western Arizona, but Buckhorn has narrower bumps (tubercles) that are four times as long as they are wide and spines that do not cover the green or purple color of the stems.

Notes: Unlike some other chollas, stem segments of Golden Cholla do not detach easily. Rather than reproducing from the rootings of fallen stems, this cactus reproduces mainly through the distribution of seeds, and therefore grows as scattered individuals as opposed to dense colonies. Golden Cholla is found in the very dry deserts of western Arizona, southeastern California, southern Nevada, and Mexico.

Spines vary in color from white to yellow and are so long and dense that they mostly obscure the green stems, making the whole cactus appear gold or silver. Sometimes called Silver Cholla. Historically, American Indians ate the fruit after carefully removing the spines.

spines

flower

fruit

Desert Christmas Cholla
Cylindropuntia leptocaulis

Size: H 2–6' (.6–1.8 m)

Shape: sprawling cactus with extremely thin, branching segmented stems

Stem: many grayish green-to-purple stem segments (joints), each 1–3" (2.5–7.5 cm) long and ⅕–¼" (.5–.6 cm) wide, with few to many spines and long, narrow, closely spaced ridges (tubercles) that are smooth and nearly inconspicuous after rain, but wrinkled in drought; segments are loosely attached

Spines: golden brown, ½–1¾" (1–4.5 cm) long

Spine Clusters: often spineless with hair-like, yellowish brown spines (glochids) in a tuft near or encircling each round area (areole) or 1 spine (rarely 3) at each junction of a branch or fruit and scattered along the stems

Flower: 1 to several delicate, pale yellow flowers alternating along the outer stems; each blossom, ½–1" (1–2.5 cm) wide, has backward-curving petals with red-tinged tips around many upright, pale yellow flower parts

Blooming: March–August and sometimes again in October; over a period of several weeks, opens around 4 o'clock in the afternoon and closes just after dark

Fruit: grape-shaped, smooth-skinned, yellowish green pod, ½" (1 cm) long, spineless but with tufts of prickles (glochids), fleshy, edible, turning bright red when ripe with tiny pale yellow seeds; fruit stays on plant throughout winter

Zone/Habitat: desert scrub, grasslands up to 5,000' (1,525 m); plateaus, along washes, slopes, canyons

Range: most of central Arizona and the southern half of the state, extending from the southeastern corner northwest through Cottonwood to north of Kingman

Desert Christmas Cholla
slimmest stem

Arizona Pencil Cholla
(pg. 187)
thicker stems,
fewer spines

Diamond-plated Pencil Cholla *(pg. 183)*
diamond-shaped bumps

Compare: Most like Arizona Pencil Cholla (pg. 187) and Diamond-plated Pencil Cholla (pg. 183), but sometimes has more spines than Arizona Pencil and long ridges rather than the diamond-shaped bumps (tubercles) of Diamond-plated Pencil.

Desert Christmas Cholla has the slimmest branches of any cactus (often less than a quarter inch), so it's not easily confused with other chollas. However, Desert Christmas hybridizes with other cholla species, and the hybrids are hard to identify. These hybrids are most common in central Arizona.

Notes: The most widespread of the cholla cacti. Its range covers about three-quarters of Arizona (except in some of the driest areas of the southwestern part of the state), half of New Mexico, two-thirds of Texas, the Arbuckle Mountains of Oklahoma, and much of northern Mexico. Almost always found growing beneath a desert tree or bush. When growing up through and supported by a tall mesquite tree, the stems can become as long as 15 feet (4.6 m).

The edible fruit is relished by birds and other desert creatures, and was eaten by Indigenous Peoples. The scarlet red color of the fruit stands out as bright relief to the eyes from the dull gray and tan hues of the desert in winter. "Christmas" in the common name refers to the time of year when the fruit ripens and perhaps to its festive appearance.

181

spines

flower

fruit

Diamond-plated Pencil Cholla

Cylindropuntia ramosissima

Size: H 2–6½' (.6–2 m)

Shape: matted and shrubby cactus with many thin, rope-like branches

Stem: multiple green or grayish green stem segments (joints), each ⅔–3" (1.6–7.5 cm) long and ¼–⅓" (.6–.8 cm) wide, with grooves outlining flattened, diamond-shaped bumps (tubercles); spines mostly on outer stems; segments are not easily detached

Spines: tan, ¾–2¼" (2–5.5 cm) long, turning purple to gray with age

Spine Clusters: up to 5 needle-like spines per cluster, but usually only 1 long spine with many minute barbs or spineless; short narrow tuft of hair-like, yellowish brown spines (glochids) next to the cluster

Flower: 1 dull yellow-to-bronzy red flower on the short side stems; each cup-shaped flower, ½" (1 cm) wide, has pointed oval petals, each with a darker middle stripe, around greenish yellow flower parts

Blooming: May–June; over a period of several weeks, but only for a couple hours each day from about noon to 2 o'clock

Fruit: densely spiny, bumpy pod, green drying to tan when mature, ⅔–1" (1.6–2.5 cm) long, containing tiny pale yellow-to-gray seeds; fruit remains on the stems for several months

Zone/Habitat: desert scrub up to 3,600' (1,100 m); along sandy washes, creosote bush flats, stony volcanic soils

Range: westernmost quarter of Arizona, from Lukeville on the Mexico border west to Yuma, north to just south of Interstate 15 in the northwestern corner of the state, and east almost to Wickenberg

Diamond-plated Pencil Cholla
crosshatched pattern on stem

Arizona Pencil Cholla
(pg. 187)
slim smooth stem

Desert Christmas Cholla
(pg. 179)
slimmer stems, smooth or wrinkled

Compare: Although similar to Arizona Pencil Cholla (pg. 187) and Desert Christmas Cholla (pg. 179), the uniquely identifying characteristic of Diamond-plated Pencil is the diamond-shaped or crosshatched pattern on its stems.

Notes: The most heat and drought tolerant of the chollas, growing in the driest, hottest deserts, where air temperatures can reach 120–125 °F (49–52 °C). The ground at these temperatures stores heat and becomes hotter than a person can bear to walk on, even with thick-soled boots. Blooms for only two hours each day, at the time when temperatures peak.

It is not picky about soil, sometimes growing on the closely interlocking rock fragments called desert pavement. The desert pavement is formed by wind removing the sand between the rocks, allowing the rocks to settle and compact. The sand swirling in the wind polishes the desert pavement.

Most reach a height of less than 3 feet (.9 m). It can lack spines altogether or have long single spines. Often found hidden low in bunch grass and too frequently first detected by an unwary hiker's shins. Very common west of Organ Pipe Cactus National Monument in southern Arizona.

185

spines

flower

fruit

Arizona Pencil Cholla
Cylindropuntia arbuscula

Size: H 2–10' (.6–3 m)

Shape: many densely branching, slim cylindrical stems hiding a short thick trunk

Stem: numerous dull green stem segments (joints), each 2½–4" (6–10 cm) long and ⅕–⅝" (.5–1.5 cm) wide, spineless or sparsely spiny; smooth, but stems wrinkle and turn yellowish green during drought

Spines: pale yellow to reddish brown, turning black with age, ⅓–1½" (.8–4 cm) long

Spine Clusters: often spineless, but with inconspicuous, hair-like, pale yellow spines (glochids) in each round area (areole); areoles are outlined with reddish brown; sometimes with 1–3 stout spines per cluster, pointing downward

Flower: 1 to several yellow blossoms (sometimes orange or bronzy red) at the tips of stems; each cup-shaped flower, 1–1¼" (2.5–5.5 cm) wide, has many rounded petals around a yellow center

Blooming: April–June; over a period of several weeks

Fruit: pear-shaped fleshy green pod, often remaining green when ripe but sometimes tinged with red, ¾–2" (2–5 cm) long, mostly spineless with reddish brown areoles; most pods are infertile; fertile pods have many pale yellow seeds

immature fruit

tiny conical leaves
on new stems

Zone/Habitat: desert scrub, sometimes in grasslands between 1,000–3,300' (305–1,010 m); usually in valleys, along washes, on flats and slopes, deep sandy soils

Range: south central Arizona, extending north almost to Payson and south to the Mexico border, and ranging to west of Lukeville and east of Sasabe

Arizona Pencil Cholla
few spines on stems

Desert Christmas Cholla
(pg. 179)
fruit turns all red

Diamond-plated Pencil Cholla *(pg. 183)*
diamond-shaped pattern on thicker stems

Compare: Similar to Desert Christmas Cholla (pg. 179), which has fruit that ripens to bright red. Diamond-plated Pencil Cholla (pg. 183) has a diamond pattern on its stems. The few spines, the almost invisible bumps on stem segments (tubercles) and the slim, smooth green stems differentiate Arizona Pencil from other cholla species, all of which are spinier, bumpier, or have thicker stems.

Notes: "Pencil" in the common name refers to the slender stem segments. Only Desert Christmas Cholla has slimmer stems.

This cactus can reach a height of 10 feet (3 m), but usually is shorter than 6 feet (1.8 m). Branching begins very close to the ground, sometimes forming impenetrable thickets. Also known as Bush Pencil Cholla.

Most of the fruit is infertile, so this cactus mainly reproduces from pieces of branches that have broken off. Almost no water is required for a stem segment to take root when it is in contact with the ground. New segments branch from segments of the previous year. Starting as buds with tiny leaves, these grow and divide during the rainy season before turning sparsely spiny.

Found only in Arizona and south into Sonora, Mexico. Readily hybridizes with Desert Christmas Cholla, Cane Cholla (pg. 195), and Staghorn Cholla (pg. 199).

spines

flower

immature fruit

Buckhorn Cholla
Cylindropuntia acanthocarpa

Size: H 3–10' (.9–3 m)

Shape: tree-like with a short woody trunk or large, bushy, and sprawling; both forms with dense or open, thin cylindrical branches

Stem: shaggy, yellowish green-to-greenish purple stem segments (joints), each 4–12" (10–30 cm) long, with many spines and broad prominent bumps (tubercles); segments are firmly attached

Spines: yellowish brown to reddish brown or gray, ½–1½" (1–4 cm) long

Spine Clusters: overlapping clusters; 6–30 spines per cluster with spines of unequal length (central spine is longest), upright or angled; lacks hair-like spines (glochids)

Flower: 1–5 blossoms (can be pink to brick red or orange to yellow) at the tips of branches; each cup-shaped flower, 2¼–3" (5.5–7.5 cm) wide, has overlapping petals with blunted, wavy edges and a center of yellow and red flower parts

Blooming: April–May; over a period of several weeks

Fruit: vase-shaped green pod, turning tan when ripe, ⅝–1¼" (1.5–3 cm) long, dry with large bumps (tubercles), densely spiny or not-so-spiny, contains a few tiny yellow-to-tan seeds

sprawling form

Zone/Habitat: desert scrub, grasslands, and juniper/pinyon pine woodlands from 500–5,000' (150–1,525 m); flats, slopes, along washes, high plateaus

Range: southwestern and central Arizona, from just northwest of Tucson through Payson and Seligman and extending north along the western edge of the state

Buckhorn Cholla
shaggy stem

Cane Cholla *(pg. 195)*
neat, tidy stem

Staghorn Cholla *(pg. 199)*
sparse spines make
tidy-looking stems

Compare: Looks a lot like Cane Cholla (pg. 195) and Staghorn Cholla (pg. 199), both of which have neat and tidy-appearing branches, while the many uneven spines of Buckhorn Cholla make its stems look shaggy. The spineless yellow fruit of Cane Cholla remains on the plant all winter, while the spiny tan fruit of Buckhorn lasts for only a few months.

Notes: A very attractive, bushy cholla with slender upright stems and large flowers that come in a variety of bright colors. Growing at low elevations, this variable cactus is tree-like in the western part of the state and short and shrubby farther east.

Indigenous Peoples of the desert Southwest traditionally gathered the unopened flower buds, steaming them for food. These buds are high in calcium and iron. Desert rodents such as kangaroo rats, pack rats, and chipmunk-like ground squirrels eat the spiny fruit and tiny seeds. Many of these animals do not need to drink water. They have specially adapted kidneys that allow them to live on the very little moisture found in dry seeds and fruit.

Buckhorn Cholla is found mostly in southern and western Arizona and the far southeastern part of California, barely extending into Utah and Nevada.

spines

flower

immature fruit

Cane Cholla
Cylindropuntia imbricata

Size: H 3–10' (.9–3 m)

Shape: compact tree-like cactus with 1 or more trunks and cylindrical branches, often drooping

Stem: multiple stem segments (joints), overall dull green to purple; each stem, 2–20" (5–50 cm) long, with even-length spines and very bumpy protuberances (tubercles); stems do not easily detach

Spines: white to gray, ⅓–¾" (.8–2 cm) long

Spine Clusters: 6–18 spines per cluster; similar-length spines

Flower: 1 to many magenta-to-purple flowers (sometimes white to yellow) at the tips of stems; each cup-shaped bloom, 1–3" (2.5–7.5 cm) wide, has many spoon-shaped petals, each with a small notch or sharp tip, and a center of yellow flower parts

Blooming: April–August; over a period of several weeks

Fruit: cylindrical, bright yellow pod, ¾–2" (2–5 cm) long, is spineless with very prominent bumps (tubercles), fleshy and contains many tiny pale yellow seeds

skeleton

Zone/Habitat: desert scrub, grasslands, oak/pinyon pine/juniper woodlands from 2,000–6,500' (610–1,980 m); slopes, canyons, and along washes

Range: southeastern quarter of Arizona, extending northwest almost to Payson; small area along Interstate 40 between Holbrook and Pinta; small area just east of Interstate 17, south of Camp Verde

Cane Cholla
similar-length spines

Buckhorn Cholla *(pg. 191)*
varying-length spines

Staghorn Cholla *(pg. 199)*
varying-length spines

Compare: Similar to Buckhorn Cholla (pg. 191) and Staghorn Cholla (pg. 199). Cane Cholla spines are overall shorter than Buckhorn and Staghorn spines and more uniform in length. Cane stems tend to droop toward the ground, and its bumps (tubercles) are closer together. The bumpy, fleshy, yellow fruit of Cane stays on the plant all winter, while Buckhorn's dry, spiny, tan fruit lasts only a few months. Cane can grow at higher elevations than the other chollas.

Notes: Cane Cholla is a very abundant cactus. Often grows out in the open, surrounded by brown grasses that make it stand out as the only green plant around. After the plant dies, the long branches dry to reveal a hollow skeletal cane, which can be used as a walking stick. Because of this, it is sometimes known as Walkingstick Cholla.

Also called Spiny Cholla for its abundant spines. The stout gray spines of similar length give the stems a fuzzy, grayish green appearance from a distance, while the vivid, lemon yellow fruit contrasts sharply when stems turn purple in winter.

Cane Cholla can endure colder temperatures than most other chollas. It grows not only in the warmer climate of Arizona, New Mexico, Texas, and northern Mexico, but can tolerate winters in Colorado, Kansas, and Oklahoma as well.

spines

flower

fruit

Staghorn Cholla
Cylindropuntia versicolor

Size: H 6–12' (1.8–3.7 m)

Shape: tree-like with a stout, woody trunk and open branches of narrow cylindrical segmented stems

Stem: many overall dull green-to-greenish purple stem segments (joints), each 1½–7" (4–18 cm) long and ½–¾" (1–2 cm) wide, with long oval bumps (tubercles) and sparse spines; slim stems are firmly attached

Spines: white or red-brown, ⅕–⁷⁄₁₀" (.5–1.8 cm) long

Spine Clusters: widely spaced clusters; 6–11 stout, slightly flattened or round spines per cluster; spines are of varying length; hair-like, orangish brown spines (glochids) in a small, crescent-shaped tuft next to each cluster

Flower: 1 to several flowers, varying from yellowish green to yellow to red to purple, at the tips of branches; each cup-shaped blossom, 1" (2.5 cm) wide, has sharp-tipped petals and yellow flower parts

Blooming: April–June; over a period of several weeks

Fruit: spineless, cone-shaped green pod, 1–1½" (2.5–4 cm) long, often on a stalk, leathery or fleshy with shallow bumps (tubercles); turning yellow tinged with purple or red when ripe and containing tiny yellow seeds; sometimes 2–3 pods form short dangling chains

Zone/Habitat: desert scrub and grasslands from 2,000–4,500' (610–1,370 m); flats, rocky slopes, canyons, along washes, and amid sandy soils

Range: south-central Arizona, especially in the area between Nogales and Florence

Staghorn Cholla
smooth fruit

Buckhorn Cholla *(pg. 191)*
spiny dry fruit

Cane Cholla *(pg. 195)*
bumpy fruit

Compare: Buckhorn Cholla (pg. 191) and Cane Cholla (pg. 195) look most like Staghorn. Buckhorn has longer, shaggier spines and spiny dry fruit that falls off in a few months, unlike the long-lasting smooth fruit of the Staghorn. Spine length of Cane is fairly uniform and Cane stems have denser bumps (tubercles) than Staghorn. Staghorn spine length varies. Its short trunk and slender stems make it look overall slimmer than Buckhorn and Cane Chollas, which have thicker branches.

Notes: Staghorn Cholla is aptly named *versicolor* for its flowers, which bloom in an astonishing variety of rich colors ranging from yellowish green to yellow to gold to coppery orange to red to magenta to purple, all with glowing yellow centers.

An abundant and tall cholla, appropriately named "Staghorn" for its open antler-like (or candelabra-like) appearance. With its upright stems branching frequently at diverse angles, this cactus gives Cactus Wrens, Curve-billed Thrashers, and other desert birds many places to nest, secure from most predators because of the spines.

The dull green stems turn purple during drought or cold. The smooth fruit is eaten on occasion by the Tohono O'odham, an Indigenous tribe.

Located in south central Arizona and south into Sonora, Mexico. Staghorn Cholla is classified by some botanists as a subspecies of Thurber Cholla, *Cylindropuntia thurberi*, which ranges throughout northern Mexico.

201

spines

flower

fruit

Jumping Cholla
Cylindropuntia fulgida

Size: H 6–15' (1.8–4.6 m)

Shape: tall and tree-like with a dark brown trunk and a crown of many thick, cylindrical branches

Stem: usually densely spiny, numerous stem segments (joints), appearing overall pale greenish yellow; each stem, 2¼–6¼" (5.5–15.5 cm) long and ¾–1" (2–2.5 cm) wide, with long spines that partially cover the pale green stems; segments detach extremely easily

Spines: pale yellow, 1" (2.5 cm) long

Spine Clusters: densely overlapping clusters; 3–12 barbed spines of greatly varying length per cluster

Flower: 1–2 delicate flowers at the tips of a few branches; each pink bloom, 1" (2.5 cm) wide, has 6–8 slightly cupped petals around a wide frilly center of many pink and cream flower parts

Blooming: April–September; opening in late afternoon and staying open throughout the night

Fruit: spineless, cone-shaped, greenish tan pod, 1–2" (2.5–5 cm) long, hanging in long, dangling clusters and remaining on the cactus for years

new stems

Zone/Habitat: desert scrub between 700–3,600' (215–1,100 m); desert flats, valleys

Range: south central Arizona, from Vicksburg on the northwest to Tubac on the southeast

Jumping Cholla
unequal-length spines

Teddy Bear Cholla *(pg. 171)*
denser, uniform-length
spines

Teddy Bear Cholla *(pg. 171)*
greenish yellow flower

Compare: Most closely resembles Teddy Bear Cholla (pg. 171), but Teddy Bear is usually shorter, has greenish yellow rather than pink flowers, denser clusters of many more spines of uniform length, and lacks chains of dangling fruit.

Notes: Jumping Cholla doesn't actually jump, but its spiny segments detach so readily that it constantly stands accused of "reaching out to touch someone." Spines have tiny, fishhook-like barbs, so whatever goes into flesh or clothing does not come out easily. Experienced desert hikers learn to carry a comb to brush the spiny stems off themselves and their pets.

Flower buds usually don't open until late afternoon, just after the height of the day's heat, when temperatures can reach 100–115 °F (38–46 °C). Most folks don't notice the small, pretty blooms since few people are out in the desert at that time.

Also called Chainfruit Cholla for the prolific, hanging, grape-like clusters of fruit. It reproduces mainly by sprouting new plants from each fallen stem segment, forming almost impenetrable forests in some areas.

spines

flower

fruit

Desert Night-blooming Cereus
Peniocereus greggii

Size: H 2–6½' (.6–2 m)

Shape: upright or sprawling cactus with long, slender, sometimes branching stems

Stem: 1 to a few, grayish green-to-grayish brown stems, 1⅓–4' (40–122 cm) long; each woody, hollow stem, ¾" (2 cm) wide and nearly square, has spine clusters along 4–6 ribs

Spines: yellowish white to gray to black, less than ¼" (.6 cm) long

Spine Clusters: widely spaced clusters on ribs; 11–15 tiny spines per cluster; spines point downward, pressed closely against the stem

Flower: 1 white blossom at the tips or sides of upright stems; each showy, fragrant flower, 2–4" (5–10 cm) wide, has long pointed petals (outer petals turn downward) around many cream flower parts

Blooming: May–July; flowers open at dusk and remain open only for a single night, until sunrise; plants in a population bloom simultaneously 3–5 times during late May to early June

Fruit: pear-shaped, bright red pod, 2½–3½" (6–9 cm) long, smooth and shiny, with sparse short spine clusters; pod turning dark brown when ripe with sweet, juicy pulp containing many tiny black seeds; fruit remains on the stem for a few months

tuber

Zone/Habitat: desert scrub and grasslands from 1,000–4,000' (305–1,220 m); flats, along washes, among creosote bushes, bursages, under mesquite and ironwood trees, silty or sandy limestone or lava soils

Range: much of the southern half of Arizona, except for the far western edge of the state

Desert Night-blooming Cereus
square stem with 4 ribs

Dahlia-rooted Cereus
round stem

Dahlia-rooted Cereus
smaller flower

Compare: Often mistaken for creosote bush branches. The only similar cactus in the United States is Dahlia-rooted Cereus, found very rarely in southern Arizona along the border with Mexico. The smaller-flowered Dahlia-rooted has 6–9 ribs on a rounded stem, not 4–6 ribs on a square stem like Desert Night-blooming Cereus.

Notes: One of fifteen *Peniocereus* species and one of two in Arizona. Stems appear dead almost year-round. Blends in with debris under branches of protective shrubs. Can grow as long as 10 feet (3 m) if supported by branches of another plant, but rarely noticed until the showy, fragrant flowers open at dusk for the night. The white glow of the blossoms attracts hawk moths, and its sweet fragrance brings in honeybees and native bees the next morning. The sucrose-rich nectar of a single flower provides enough energy to a hawk moth for 3–20 minutes of hovering flight. Sometimes called Queen of the Night for its beautiful flowers.

This cactus has a large underground tuber that can grow as big as a basketball and weigh from 15–90 pounds (6.8–41 kg). Historically, Indigenous Peoples dug the tuber to use for food and treating illness. Today, large populations of this cactus have been exterminated by collectors. Some elderly residents of Tucson talk of seeing as many as 100 blossoms open on a single cactus, before collectors removed the largest plants. Propagated easily from short stem cuttings and from seed.

spines

flower

immature fruit

Organic Pipe Cactus
Stenocereus thurberi

Size: H 9–20' (2.7–6.1 m), some up to 40' (12.2 m)

Shape: large clusters of tall columns of stems branching from the base

Stem: yellowish green or dull green stems, each 8" (20 cm) wide, with 15–19 rounded vertical ribs lined with spines

Spines: reddish brown, aging to gray with dark tips, ½–2½" (1–6 cm) long

Spine Clusters: non-overlapping clusters spaced ½" (1 cm) apart on ribs; each cluster has 11–14 spines that look alike yet can be different lengths, such as the longer central spines and shorter radial spines, and also has felt-like reddish hairs

Flower: white blossoms in a loose ring below top of stems; each funnel-shaped flower, 2½–3" (6–7.5 cm) wide, has petals with pink midstripes and a pale yellow center; bloom is held by a long green tube of short, scale-like, red-tipped green leaves (bracts)

Blooming: April–July; flowers open after sunset and close soon after sunrise the next morning

Fruit: spiny green pod, 2–2½" (5–6 cm) long, with a pinkish tuft of dry flower parts on top; fruit loses it red and black spines and turns red when ripe, containing sweet red pulp with glossy dark brown seeds

immature Organ Pipe Cactus

Zone/Habitat: desert scrub below 2,000' (610 m); bajadas, ridges, south-facing rocky hillsides

Range: south central Arizona, including Lukeville and Ajo to the west and Marana to the east

Organ Pipe Cactus
pink-tinged flower

Saguaro *(pg. 219)*
waxy white flowers

Senita Cactus *(pg. 215)*
beard-like gray spines
top older stems

Compare: Organ Pipe has pink-tinged flowers, not waxy white flowers like Saguaro (pg. 219). Much like Senita Cactus (pg. 215), but lacks beard-like gray spines on its upper stems.

Notes: The Organ Pipe Cactus National Monument in southern Arizona was established to protect this unique species. Branches into several dozen columnar stems that taper to rounded tips, resembling organ pipes. Limited from ranging farther north by its susceptibility to temperatures below 25 °F (-4 °C). Stems in Arizona are often irregularly segmented due to tip damage caused by cold weather. Widespread in warmer Mexico.

Blossoms open in summer and are pollinated by the nectar-feeding Long-nosed Bat, which literally grabs its sweet drinks on the fly. The Tohono O'odham People, an Indigenous tribe residing east of Organ Pipe Cactus National Monument, gather the fruit to make a syrup for jelly and wine. They also dry the fruit, saving the pulp and seeds to eat during winter months.

A young Organ Pipe plant needs shade and shelter from the cold and hungry animals. Larger "nurse" plants, such as ironwood and palo verde trees and bursages, provide this defense for young seedlings. Mature Organ Pipe cacti have a large shallow system of roots that absorbs all available water, which in turn kills the nurse plant—a poor reward for such protection.

spines

flower

fruit

Senita Cactus
Pachycereus schottii

Size: H 10–20' (3–6.1 m)

Shape: large upright clusters of up to 100 hexagonal stems branching at the ground

Stem: yellowish green stems, each 4–8" (10–20 cm) wide, with 5–6 prominent ribs and thick, waxy, or leathery skin; upper stems with long spines in beard-like tufts that obscure the stem color; ribs on lower stems lined with widely spaced spine clusters

Spines: gray to black, 1½–4" (4–10 cm) long, on upper parts of stems; pinkish red, aging to gray with dark tips, less than 1" (2.5 cm) long, on lower portions of stems

Spine Clusters: 15–50 long, flat, corkscrew-like spines in dense clusters on upper parts of older, tall stems; 7–10 short stout spines per cluster on lower portions of stems and on younger stems

Flower: cream-colored blooms, turning light pink, just above the spine clusters on south-facing sides of stems; each short, funnel-shaped flower, 1½" (4 cm) wide, has white flower parts and is held by a pinkish green stem made up of long pointed leaves (bracts)

Blooming: mostly May–June, but anytime from spring through fall; flowers open at dusk and close midmorning the next day

Fruit: spineless, fleshy, oval green pod, 1–1½" (2.5–4 cm) long, turning red when ripe with sour, but edible, red pulp containing black seeds

Zone/Habitat: desert scrub up to 1,500' (460 m); flats, valleys, and other areas with deep, sandy soils

Range: found in a tiny area of southwestern Arizona, along the border with Mexico

Senita Cactus
beard-like gray spines
on upper part of stem

Organ Pipe Cactus (pg. 211)
no extra spines atop
stems

Saguaro (pg. 219)
white flowers at the top
of stem

Compare: Much like Organ Pipe Cactus (pg. 211), but Senita has beard-like spines on its upper stems. Senita's cream-to-pink flowers grow only on the sides of stems, unlike Saguaro (pg. 219) and Organ Pipe flowers, which usually grow at or near the stem tips.

Notes: This cactus grows in clusters of many stems topped with long, flexible gray spines. "Senita" is Spanish for "old" and refers to the similarity of the beard-like gray spines to the beard of an old man. The genus *Pachycereus* means "thick wax candle," referring to the thick waxy skin and shape of the stems. Some naturalists think the stems resemble a giant bottlebrush more than a candle. The species name *schottii* honors Arthur Schott, a naturalist for the Mexico Boundary Commission in the 1800s.

Flowers bloom for only a night, mainly in the spring. In Arizona populations, blossoms open 10 minutes after sunset. The Senita Cactus and pyralid moths have a mutually beneficial relationship. About 90 percent of Senita blossoms are pollinated by female pyralids. Using specialized scales on their abdomens, they collect the pollen and deposit it on the stigma of the next flower. Pyralid moth larvae eat only the seeds of the Senita. Oddly, ants feed on nectar secreted by spine clusters and protect the plant from being eaten by other insects.

Easily seen in Senita Basin of Organ Pipe Cactus National Monument near Lukeville. More widespread in Mexico.

spines

flower

fruit

Saguaro
Carnegiea gigantea

Size: H 10–30' (3–9.1 m), some 40–50' (12.2–15 m)

Shape: large, telephone pole-like stem with branching, gracefully curved arms

Stem: upright dull green stem, 10–30" (25–76 cm) wide, lined with 19–26 thick ribs topped with spines

Spines: straight stout spines, off-white to gray with dark tips, ½–2" (1–5 cm) long; after 50 years, spines on new portions of arms are straw-colored and bristle-like

Spine Clusters: spaced ½" (1 cm) apart along ribs, with 15–28 spines per cluster; each cluster has 4–7 longer central spines among slimmer radial spines

Flower: large waxy white blossoms cluster near the stem tips; each funnel-shaped flower, 5" (13 cm) long and 2½–3½" (6–9 cm) wide, has wavy edges and a pale yellow and white center; bloom held by a long tube of pointed green leaves (bracts)

Blooming: late April–early June; over a period of several weeks; flowers open 2 hours after sunset and remain open until the next afternoon

Fruit: elliptical green pod, 2–4" (5–10 cm) long, with a brown tuft of dry flower parts on top, turns red and splits open when ripe, revealing juicy red pulp with small black seeds

crested form

skeleton

immature Saguaro

Zone/Habitat: desert scrub and grasslands between 600–4,600' (180–1,400 m); flats, arroyos, rocky ridges, south-facing hillsides, bajadas, canyons

Range: southwestern and south central Arizona, ranging over about a third of the state, from Needles on the California border to Sasabe on the Mexico border to just southwest of Safford in the eastern part of the state

Saguaro
straight central spines

Fishhook Barrel *(pg. 107)*
curved central spines

Compass Barrel *(pg. 111)*
shorter plant, with a
barrel shape

Compare: A tall Fishhook Barrel (pg. 107) looks like a young Saguaro, but has hooked central spines. All barrel cacti, such as Compass Barrel (pg. 111), have a barrel shape. Organ Pipe Cactus (pg. 211) and Senita Cactus (pg. 215) branch into multiple stems from the base, not higher up from a central trunk.

Notes: The tallest and largest cactus in Arizona. Slow growing, taking 15 years to reach a foot tall and 50–75 years to grow its first arm. A massive cactus when 100–200 years old, towering over desert trees. Can have up to 30 arms and weigh several tons due to the mass of the water in the pulpy interior. A ring of woody, rod-like stalks inside supports the liquid weight and remains upright after the plant dies. Made mostly of water, this giant is sensitive to freezing, thus it is limited to areas that never have periods of 24 hours or more below 32 °F (0 °C). During monsoons, the stem swells with absorbed rain-water and ribs widen and flatten like accordion folds. Ribs are close together and grooves are deep when cactus is stressed by drought. The cause of a rare, crested growth form is unknown.

The blossoms of Arizona's state flower attract nectar-feeding bats. Elf Owls, the smallest owls in the world, raise their young in Saguaro nest cavities. These dry, boot-shaped cavities are 10–30 feet (3–9.1 m) above the ground and 20 degrees cooler than outside summer air temperatures. Seen in dense forests of Saguaro National Park near Tucson.

The desert plants included in this section will help you identify four other drought-tolerant plants in Arizona that superficially look like cacti, but are not. All of these species differ from cacti by their lack of areoles—the cushiony structures on stems where flowers and spines develop. Unlike cacti, these arid-climate plants have long-lasting leaves or they lack succulent stems and many long spines. In addition, they produce small flowers in clusters that do not resemble the large flowers of cacti. These are all native plants that can be found in the wild, but also are seen in landscape plantings of the Southwest.

Common Sotol
Dasylirion wheeleri

10–15' (3–4.6 m)

There are four sotol species in the United States, but only the **Common Sotol** occurs in Arizona, ranging over the southern half of the state. Like other sotols, Common Sotol has thin, flat, tough leaves with pointed tips and fishhook-like thorns lining the edges. Sometimes forms a short trunk. Sends up a tall flower stalk each summer that produces clusters of bottlebrush-shaped yellow flowers. Occasionally confused with agaves and yuccas.

flower

Ocotillo
Fouquieria splendens

6–20' (1.8–6.1 m)

The **Ocotillo** has spines on woody stems and is a relative of the Boojumtree of Mexico. The spines are modified primary leaves that drop from their leafstalks, which then become sharply pointed and woody. Lacking leaves or blooms and appearing dead most of the year, the gray-brown woody stems resemble a fan-shaped garden trellis made of spiny sticks. When spring comes, its flowers bud and open, often before the appearance of leaves, with flame-shaped orange-red flower clusters blossoming atop each long thin stem.

Agave
Agave spp.

10–20' (3–6.1 m)

Arizona has more than a dozen agave species occurring in all parts of the state. While drought tolerant and prickly like cacti, the **Agave** is more closely related to plants in the Lily and Amaryllis families. It is a succulent with thick leathery leaves that grow in a rosette, usually as tall as 12–36 inches (30–91 cm). Leaves are slow-growing, sharply pointed, and often have small teeth along the edges. Rising from middle of the rosette only once in a plant's lifetime, a tall branching flower stalk bears clusters of small, tubular, yellow blossoms that are open during the day. After blooming, the plant dies. Often called Century Plant because historically it was believed the plant lived a hundred years before blooming and dying.

Soaptree Yucca
Yucca elata
20–30' (6.1–9.1 m)

Soaptree Yucca is a tree-like plant with one or more trunks branching in graceful upsweeping arms. Blade-like, thorny-edged leaves are 3–4 feet (91–122 cm) long and a mere ½ inch (1 cm) wide and laced with white fibers. Bell-shaped white flowers grow in spike clusters above the leaves on stalks 4–6 feet (1.2–1.8 m) tall and bloom from May through July, but only every few years. In Arizona there are eight yucca species, all with similar-looking white flowers.

The well-known Joshua Tree is a yucca found in the Mojave Desert. Ranges from California, Nevada, and Utah to northwestern Mexico and can be seen in Arizona between the towns of Wickenburg and Wikieup, along a route which is called the Joshua Tree Parkway of Arizona.

GLOSSARY

Anther: A part of the male flower that contains the pollen.

Areole: The round or oval, partly raised, cushiony point of attachment of cactus spines to the stem of the plant.

Arm: A curved or bent branch of a cactus growing from the trunk, as in Saguaro.

Arroyo: A usually dry and sandy streambed in the Southwest over which water flows during or after heavy rains. See *wash*.

Bajadas: Broad fan-like folds of sand, earth, and rocks on the lower slopes of desert mountains, deposited by the erosive action of streams or washes.

Bract: A leaf-like structure usually found at the base of a flower.

Branch: A supporting part of a plant growing from the trunk or other branches and usually bearing the leaves or flowers. See *stem*.

Central spine: One of the inner, larger, and longer major spines of a spine cluster, usually pointing out from the cactus stem, sometimes with a hooked tip.

Cluster: A group or collection of spines, flowers, or fruit.

Creosote bush: A yellow-flowered evergreen bush with a resinous odor, most strongly fragrant after rainfall, abundant in Southwest deserts.

Ephemeral: Lasting for only a short time each spring.

Flower: To bloom, or produce a flower or flowers as a means of reproduction.

Fruit: A ripened ovary or reproductive structure that contains one or more seeds, such as a pod.

Glochid: One of the tiny, hair-like barbed spines or bristles found in tufts in the spine clusters of cacti such as prickly pears and chollas.

Joint: A segment or section of a stem, found only in cholla and prickly pear cacti. See *pad*.

Mesa: An elevated, flat expanse of land (plateau), with one or more steep sides or cliffs; Spanish for "tableland."

Nurse plant: A mature plant that shelters seedlings from weather.

Pad: A flat, paddle-shaped stem segment of prickly pear cacti. See *joint*.

Petal: A basic flower part that is usually brightly colored, serving to attract pollinating insects.

Photosynthesis: In green plants, the conversion of water and carbon dioxide into carbohydrates (food) from energy in sunlight.

Pistil: The female part of a flower made up of an ovary, style, and stigma, often in the center of the flower.

Pod: A fruit that contains many seeds, as in Cane Cholla.

Pollination: The transfer of pollen from the male anther to the female stigma, usually resulting in the production of seeds.

Radial spine: One of the outermost spines of a cluster, radiating around and spreading out from the longer, thicker central spines.

Rib: An outward vertical or wavy fold of the surface of a cactus stem, usually bearing clusters of spines.

Riparian deciduous: A life zone that lies within other life zones, but only near streams or intermittently running washes, where new cactus seedlings flourish during long periods of drought.

Sepal: A member of the outermost set of petals of a flower, typically green or leafy, but often colored and resembling a petal.

Spine: A stiff, sharply pointed woody outgrowth on a cactus. See *thorn*.

Spine cluster: A group of spines in each areole of a cactus stem, usually including radial and central spines.

Stamen: The male parts of a flower, consisting of an anther and a filament.

Stem: An elongated supporting part of a plant growing from the root or branching from the trunk. See *branch*.

Stigma: The female part of the flower that receives pollen.

Succulent: A plant that has thick, water-storing leaves or stems, such as a cactus or agave.

Taproot: The primary, vertically descending root of a plant.

Thorn: A stiff, usually long and sharply pointed woody outgrowth from a stem, as in Common Sotol. See *spine*.

Trunk: The main stem or body of a tree or tree-like cactus, often woody and usually supporting branches.

Tubercle: A knobby projection on a cactus stem, as in Buckhorn Cholla.

Tuna: Spanish for the edible fruit of a prickly pear cactus.

Wash: A usually dry and sandy streambed in the Southwest over which water flows during or after heavy rains. See *arroyo*.

Woody: Having the appearance of wood, as in stems, trunks, and spines.

CHECK LIST/INDEX *Use the boxes to check cacti you've seen.*

PHOTO CREDITS

All photos are copyright of their respective photographers as of 2023.

Rick and Nora Bowers: 22 (all), 24, 25 (all), 26 (all), 28, 29 (all), 30 (all), 32, 33 (all), 34 (main, spines, fruit), 36 (both), 37 (all), 38 (all), 40, 41 (all), 42 (main, spines, fruit), 44 (both), 45 (all), 46 (all), 48, 49 (all), 50 (all), 52 (both), 53 (all), 54 (spines), 56 (both), 57 (all), 58 (main, spines, flower), 60 (both), 61 (all), 62 (spines), 64, 65 (all), 66 (all), 68, 69 (all), 70 (main, spines, flower), 73 (all), 74 (spines, fruit), 76, 77 (left, middle), 78 (main, spines, flower), 80, 81 (all), 82 (all), 85 (left, middle), 86 (all), 88, 89 (all), 90 (main, spines, flower), 92, 93 (right), 94 (main, spines, flower), 96, 97 (all), 98 (main, spines), 100, 101 (all), 102 (fruit), 104 (gray notch), 105 (all), 106 (all), 108, 109 (all), 110 (all), 112 (both), 113 (all), 117 (middle, right), 118 (main, spines, fruit), 121 (all), 122 (all), 124 (both), 125 (all), 126 (all), 128, 129 (all), 130 (main, spines), 132, 133 (left, right), 134 (flower, fruit), 137 (all), 138 (all), 140 (both), 141 (all), 142 (main, spines, fruit), 144, 145 (all), 146 (all), 148, 149 (all), 150 (all), 152 (all), 153 (all), 154 (main, spines), 156 (all), 157 (all), 158 (all), 160, 161 (all), 162 (main, spines, fruit), 165 (all), 166 (all), 168, 169 (left, middle), 170 (all), 172 (both), 173 (all), 174 (main, spines, flower), 176 (both), 177 (all), 178 (all), 181 (all), 182 (main, spines, fruit), 184, 185 (all), 186 (all), 188 (all), 189 (all), 190 (all), 192 (both), 193 (all), 194 (all), 196 (both), 197 (all), 198 (all), 200, 201 (all), 202 (main, flower), 204 (both), 205 (all), 206 (all), 208 (main), 209 (left), 210 (spines, flower, fruit), 213 (all), 214 (main, spines, flower), 217 (all), 218 (all), 220 (all), 221 (all), 222, 223 (both), 225

Michael L. Charters: 130 (flower)

Cpifbg13/Shutterstock.com: 42 (flower)

Mark A. Dimmitt/Arizona-Sonora Desert Museum: 154 (flower), 169 (right), 174 (fruit)

Erik F. Enderson: 54 (fruit), 58 (fruit), 90 (fruit)

Alan English: 180

Dominic Gentilcore PhD/Shutterstock.com: 62 (main)

Mary Ellen Harte: 117 (left)

Stephen Ingram: 130 (fruit)

Lori Jacobson: 70 (fruit)

Matthew B. Johnson: 54 (main, flower), 72, 74 (main, flower), 77 (right), 84, 93 (left, middle), 102 (flower), 104 (main), 116 (both), 118 (flower), 120, 133 (middle), 136, 142 (flower), 162 (flower), 164, 209 (middle, right), 212

Eric Kiefer: 114 (fruit)

Gary A. Monroe: 62 (flower), 182 (flower)

Jerry Murray: 114 (flower)

reisegraf.ch/Shutterstock.com: 210 (main)

Jim Rorabaugh: 34 (flower), 78 (fruit)

S. Rutman: 208 (tuber), 214 (fruit)

Phillip Ruttenbur: 85 (right), 94 (fruit)

Al Schneider: 114 (spines)

Bill Sullivan: 98 (flower)

Stan Tekiela: 102 (main, spines), 104 (fruit), 134 (main, spines), 202 (spines, fruit), 224

Charles Webber/California Academy of Sciences: 154 (fruit)

Jeffrey Wickey/Shutterstock.com: 216

Dorde Woodruff: 114 (main)

www.birdandhike.com: 98 (fruit)

ABOUT THE AUTHORS

Nora Mays Bowers

Nora Mays Bowers is a writer and nature photographer. She likes being in nature and looking at birds, wildlife, and plants. Long ago, she earned a Master of Science degree in Ecology from the University of Arizona. She is the primary author of *Wildflowers of Arizona, Wildflowers of the Carolinas, Wildflowers of Texas, Cactus of Texas, Cactus of the Southwest,* and *Kaufman Focus Guides: Mammals of North America*. Most of the photographs in all these guides were taken by her and her husband, Rick Bowers.

Rick Bowers

Rick Bowers began birding at age ten while living on Ft. Huachuca, Arizona. In less than a year he was leading birders to the specialty birds of Southeastern Arizona. During high school and college, he led individuals and groups on tours in southeastern Arizona. For 16 years after college Rick led birdwatching tours for Victor Emanuel Nature Tours. Now when not working on books or photography, Rick leads photography and birding tours around the world through his company, Bowers Birding & Photo Safaris.

Stan Tekiela

Naturalist, wildlife photographer, and writer Stan Tekiela is the originator of the popular state-specific field guide series that includes the *Birds of Arizona Field Guide.* Stan has authored more than 190 educational books, including field guides, quick guides, nature books, children's books, and more, presenting many species of animals and plants.

With a Bachelor of Science degree in natural history from the University of Minnesota and as an active professional naturalist for more than 30 years, Stan studies and photographs wildlife throughout the United States and Canada. He has received national and regional awards for his books and photographs and is also a well-known columnist and radio personality. His syndicated column appears in more than 25 newspapers, and his wildlife programs are broadcast on a number of Midwest radio stations. You can follow Stan on Facebook and Twitter or contact him via his website, naturesmart.com.